Selected Writings on

THE AWARENESS PRINCIPLE

Selected writings on:

THE AWARENESS PRINCIPLE

A radical new philosophy of life, science and religion

New expanded edition 2008

Acharya Peter Wilberg

First published 2007 by
Exposure Publishing,
an imprint of
Diggory Press Ltd.

This edition published 2008 by
New Yoga Publications,
an imprint of
New Gnosis Publications

© Peter Wilberg 2007

British Library Cataloguing In Publication Data
A Record of this Publication is available
from the British Library

ISBN 978-1-904519-09-6

Mantram

The pure Awareness of any self, identity, body, world or universe

Transcends every self, identity, body, world or universe -

Yet pervades and takes shape as them all.

Note to the Reader

The project of achieving an ever-more precise exposition of what I call 'The Awareness Principle' – the understanding of Awareness itself as the singular and ultimate reality behind and within all things - is an on-going and evolving one. As a result, I have found myself formulating new expositions of this Principle – and the 'Practices of Awareness' that follow from it - in different contexts or in what appear to be only slightly adjusted terms. This work is a second anthology of such expositions or 'selected writings' on The Awareness Principle' - taken from a variety of earlier essays and books. Consequently however, many of the texts it contains may seem repetitious in their message or even near-identical in their phrasing and wording. In asking for the reader's tolerance here, I can only remark that even the slightest of differences in wording and context between the texts included in this volume - as well as the element of repetition itself – may be useful in reinforcing the reader's understanding of its message. And just as the One singular reality behind all realities can take countless forms, so is there *no end* to the ways in which a single principle and its practice – not least one which seeks to give expression to that One reality and offer a direct experience of it - can be refined and re-thought.

Acharya Peter Wilberg 2008

"... awareness qua awareness [is] not awareness as a topic within, or relative to, *a context that defines it by confining* it, as e.g. social awareness, physical awareness or awareness physically analysed ... Rather, without trepidation, awareness 'itself' – awareness without confinement – is our topic; awareness without imposed limits as our 'context'... Awareness as such is a truly primitive term, unlike 'consciousness' (with all its differentiated levels) which ... always refers to being 'aware-of-something', of some content, as vivid or vague, sharp or dim as it may be. Awareness ... belongs to no one exclusively, has no restrictions, derivations or explanations ... *just is*. Awareness is a singularity beyond personality and impersonality – which cannot be contained, curtailed, expanded or transcended from 'without awareness'. It is not as important to simply label this awareness with a word like God, the Absolute or what have you, as to *submit* and *abandon* yourself to this singularity of awareness ... the awareness that runs *through* you as one person *of* a multi-personal universe of unlimited awareness ... [This] 'spiritual' awareness cannot be locked up in churches, temples and mosques ... from which imposing directives issue forth, nor can it thrive diluted as part of the mainstream culture it is supposed to be educating."

Michael Kosok - 'The Singularity of Awareness'

"Now thinking which constructs a world of objects understands these objects; but meditative thinking begins with an awareness of the field within which these objects are ... the field of awareness itself."

John Anderson (translator of Martin Heidegger's 'Discourse on Thinking')

The most fundamental scientific 'fact' is not the existence of a universe of things in space and time but *awareness* of such a universe.

We can no more explain awareness *as such* by any 'thing' we are *aware of* than we can explain *dreaming* as such by something we *dream of.*

Awareness is nothing in need of scientific 'explanation'. For by its very nature it is no 'thing', and thus not explainable by some other thing.

Awareness is not a 'thing' that can evolve from or arise out of an unaware or insentient universe of things. On the contrary all things in the universe emerge and take shape out of a *universal awareness.*

Everything and everyone is a portion and expression of the universal awareness that we call 'God'. God is not a person, but all persons are *personifications* of the universal awareness that is God.

Everything and everyone is a shape taken *by* the universal awareness *within* that awareness.

Awareness is everything. Everything is an awareness.

Awareness is nothing enclosed within our bodies or brains. It is the very *space* within which we experience all things – including our bodies themselves.

Peter Wilberg

CONTENTS

PREFACE

Taking Time to Be Aware

Today's world faces a grave economic, ecological, cultural crisis – indeed a global civilisational crisis. The word 'crisis' means a 'turning point' in time. The basic need expressed in this crisis is for human beings to find a way of *being-in-time* that is not simply dominated by 'busy-ness', by *doing*, and aimed only at *having*. The new relation to time that human beings so desperately need at this time is one in which they give themselves time, not just to produce or consume, work or play – but to *be aware*. For to truly 'be' *is* to *be aware*. Just as to truly 'meditate' is simply to *take time to be aware*. For only by taking *time* to be aware can each of us open up a broader *space* of awareness - one which, like the clear and empty space surrounding things, allows us to meditate, place in perspective and come to new insights regarding whatever questions, concerns or feelings are currently addressing us. Only out of such a *broader*, more spacious and expansive awareness *field* can human beings also come to *deeper*, more thoughtful decisions and find better practical solutions to both personal and world problems. And only out of this broadened and deepened awareness can we also relate to other human beings in a more meditative and aware way – thus bringing about a healing transformation in human relations.

All mismanagement, misgovernment and mistreatment of others stem from the self-defeating rush of busy-ness that characterises our global business culture. This is a culture of enforced economic conscription of *all* ('full employment') which ends up rendering the unique awareness, potentials and creativity of *each* more or less wholly *unemployed*. The value our global capitalist culture places on activity, speed and busy-ness denies the time needed for meditative and aware decision-making - but in this way also slows down or entirely blocks *truly aware, thoughtful and effective action*. Behind this culture is a deep-seated fear of awareness, not least awareness of all the ways in which - lacking awareness - human beings are destroying each other and the earth.

The resulting global crisis and turning point in time that we now face tells us that it is high time for humanity to become more aware, high time for a cultural revolution in awareness - one based not just on 'slowing down' but on cultivating a whole new way of aware experiencing and action, living and relating, thinking and feeling. This in turn requires new forms of *education in awareness* in all areas of life and knowledge - and not just education in facts or skills. Above all it requires a new understanding of awareness as something essentially distinct from mere consciousness 'of' things. There is all that we experience, all that occurs or goes on in ourselves and the world. And there is *the awareness* of all that occurs or goes on – *the awareness* of all we experience. That awareness - awareness 'as such' or 'pure awareness' - is what alone can free human beings from bondage to anything they are conscious or aware *of*.

Awareness *as such* is a not a product of the brain, bounded by our bodies, or the mere private property of individuals or groups. Instead is has an essentially unbounded and universal character. It is the 'trans-personal' dimension of consciousness. As such, it transcends *identity* – as it also transcends all group *identifications* – social and economic, ethnic, cultural and religious. For awareness itself is the essence of the divine - one and indivisible. That is why anyone who cultivates awareness works not only for their own well-being but for that of the world - a world whose ills all result from a lack of awareness, and thus can never be healed through the politics or psychology of *identity*.

OPENING VERSES

Awareness as Absolute Principle

How do you know that anything at all exists?

Only out of an Awareness of things.

How do you know that you yourself exist?

Only out of an Awareness of existing - of being.

How do you know there is a world?

Only from within a world of Awareness.

How do you know you have a body or self?

Only out of an Awareness of body and self.

What comes first then -

All you are aware of, or

Awareness as such?

Awareness as such

Is distinct – in principle – from each

And every thing or world, being or body

That we are aware 'of'.

It cannot – in principle – be reduced

To the property or product of any thing or world,

Being or body that we are aware *of.*

This absolute axiom or principle is

'The Awareness Principle'.

Awareness as Ultimate Reality

If 'Spirit' is not
Some 'thing' like any other,
Then what exactly is it?

If 'God' is not some 'being'
Among others, or like any other,
Then what or who exactly is it?

If 'Energy' is not some
Material 'thing' like any other
Then what exactly is it?

Awareness,
Like 'Spirit', 'God' or 'Energy'
Is certainly 'no thing' and 'no being'
Yet that does not mean that
It is 'nothing' or
'Non-being'.

For without Awareness,
How could there ever be an awareness, not only of
Any thing or being in the world, but even
Of what we call 'Spirit', 'God' or 'Energy'?

This principle makes Awareness as such
The Ultimate Reality behind all All That Is, and
The essence of 'Spirit', 'God' and 'Energy'.

Awareness as Field Consciousness

If people get lost in
Any form of activity or experiencing,
Whether thinking or talking, watching TV,
Engaging in their work or in everyday chores,
Worrying about their life, or just feeling particular
Emotions, sensations, pains or pleasures,
Then though they are 'conscious',
They are not Aware.

Thus you may be 'conscious'
Of making yourself a cup of coffee.
Yet how aware are you of your whole body and of
Your breathing as you do so, of your every accompanying
Thought and feeling, and of the feel of each object you handle?
And how aware are you of the other things and people in the
Space around you as you 'consciously'
Make your cup of coffee?

Similarly, you may be
'Conscious' of what you are seeing on TV
Or what you are hearing another person say.
Yet how aware are you of your own body
As you do so, of other objects in the
Room besides the TV, and of the
Whole body of the person
As they speak?

> Whenever our attention gets
> Focussed or fixated on any one thing
> We are experiencing or 'conscious' of,
> We lose Awareness.

Unlike ordinary 'consciousness',
Awareness is not focussed on any
One thing that we happen to be aware OF.
Awareness is more like the clear space
Surrounding us and all things
We experience within it;
Inseparable and yet
Distinct from them.

> 'Consciousness' is merely
> 'Ego-awareness' or 'focal awareness',
> Focussed on or identified with some
> Element of our experience.

Awareness is more than ordinary consciousness,
More than just 'ego awareness' or 'focal awareness'.
Instead it is a vast, universal Consciousness Field,
A Field Consciousness that embraces and pervades
Each and every thing we are aware of within it, whilst
Remaining absolutely distinct from them all -
A Divine-Universal Consciousness Field.

Awareness as Perception

Where do you actually experience
The things you perceive in the world around you?
Do you ever experience these perceptions
'In' your eyes or ears, head or brain?

Do you ever experience your brain
Making images of things from signals
Sent through nerves by your sense organs,
In the way that science describes?

Or do you experience perceptions
Of things in the world there, where they are -
'Out there' in the space around them, and not
'In here' - in your body or brain?

If so, has it ever occurred to you
That AWARENESS of objects 'out there'
In the very the space surrounding your body,
Cannot be something locked up 'in' your body,
'In' your eyes or ears, head or brain?

In reality that Awareness
Pervades the entire world-space around your body,
Which is nothing but a spacious field
OF Awareness.

All perceptions, actual or potential, of
Things 'out there' in the world, arise and occur
Within this field or world-space of Awareness and
Not 'through' your senses or 'in' your brain.
Awareness is not 'in here' but 'out there',
Just where you perceive things to be.

As in entering a great temple or
Standing in a wonderful landscape,
It is only if we first of all take time to sense
The entire spacious field of awareness around us, that we can
Not only 'perceive' the various things in it but FEEL them,
Letting ourselves touch and be touched,
Like by a great sculpture or tree, by their
Sheer presence within that field.

It is not with 'sense organs' that
Perception begins, but with our very skins -
That organ of whole-body sensing by which alone
We can sense the spacious field of awareness
In which all things first come to be and
Be perceived in every detail.

We are not aware because we can
Perceive things through our sense organs.
We can perceive things only because
Because the arise and abide
In a field of Awareness.

Awareness as Space

Without space – space as such
There could be no awareness of anything IN space.

Similarly, without awareness – awareness as such,
There could be no awareness 'of' anything at all …

… No awareness of a universe, of galaxies and planets,
Of the things around you, of your body or yourself.

"Space - the final frontier…"
Yet does our understanding of the mysteries of outer space
Really depend on how far we can peer into it with eyes or instruments,
Or how far we can journey into its furthest reaches with spaceships?

Space is not 'the final frontier' because it is no frontier at all.
For like awareness - and God - space is One, singular and indivisible.
To understand and experience the true nature of 'God' you need do no
More than understand and experience the true nature of space.

Then again, space is 'the final frontier' – but a frontier of
Understanding and experience and not of scientific exploration.
The understanding that awareness as such is something that can
No more be bounded by our bodies than the expanse of space.

The truth is that space is awareness - that universal field of
Awareness without which we could not be aware of any thing or
Universe at all - and that is identical with what we call God.

Awareness is not something encapsulated within us.
We dwell within awareness as we dwell within space,
To experience 'empty' space itself as the divine-universal
Awareness within which we dwell – that is truth.

Awareness as Time

Do you often feel you are always 'on the move',
Going from one thing or place to another.
Dealing with one thing 'after' another,
Without any breathing space?

Have you noticed how feeling that
You have no 'space' for yourself
Goes together with feeling you have
No time for yourself, or for others?

Have you noticed how feeling that
You have no 'time' for yourself
Goes together with feeling you have
No space for yourself, or for others?

Yet by granting yourself even the shortest
Time to stop 'doing' and just be aware
Of all that was or is preoccupying you,
You will feel that you have more 'space'.

You do not need to go from one thing to another
In time, or one place to another in space, in order
To experience an expanded time-space of awareness
That embraces your past, present and future.

All you need do is stop doing - whether for
Seconds, minutes or hours - and give yourself
Time to Be Aware of all that is currently just filling,
Preoccupying and contracting your awareness space.

All you need do is to give yourself breathing spaces after
Each and every activity you engage in, spaces in which, by
Giving yourself TIME to be Aware, not least of your breathing itself,
You will begin - quite literally – to feel yourself breathing the
Blissful 'airiness' of a clearer more spacious Awareness.

Time and space are not dimensions of
The physical universe but of Awareness.
Space is what makes space for things to
Abide, occur or come to presence in awareness.

Time itself is not a one-dimensional line but a
Vast, voluminous Space of awareness, encompassing
All that is occurring or coming to presence, not only
In your present, but in your past and future too.

Awareness as Matter

What are sounds and colours, sounds and colours of...?
What are brightness and darkness qualities of...?
What are lightness and heaviness qualities of...?
What are warmth and coolness qualities of...?
What is 'material' solidity a quality of ...?
Of 'Matter' or of sensory Awareness?

Matter is not made up of
Multitudes of invisible particles.
It is made up of all such potential qualities of
Subjective, sensory awareness.

What we experience
As 'material' or 'physical'
And not merely imaginary,
Is anything that we know we can
Not only see or hear, but also
Potentially touch and feel,
Taste and smell.

Matter is no 'thing in itself'.
Indeed it is no 'thing' at all, but
Made up of all those potential qualities of
Sensory awareness, visual, aural or tactile,
That complement the actual qualities
Of things that we experience.

Matter is the great 'mother' or
'Mater' of all things, the pure potential for
Sensory experiencing latent in the larger
Field of sensory awareness.
We call space-time.

The soul of matter is the
Matter of soul, of Pure Awareness -
Its infinite potentialities and power of
Manifestation and materialisation.
Immaterial 'Spirit' – Awareness,
Is precisely that which Matters -
Materialising itself
As all things.

Awareness as Meditation

If we are not aware of our thoughts AS thoughts,
We identify and confuse them with the very things or people
That we are thinking about - forgetting that
Thoughts 'about' reality are not reality.

'Meditation' means
Entering and sustaining a state
Of calm, clear, thought-free awareness.
Yet we need not seek to 'stop' thinking
Or to 'empty' our heads of thoughts
In order to attain this state.
In order to 'meditate'.

For just as the Awareness of a thing
Is not itself a 'thing' we can see, touch or hold,
So also is the Awareness of a thought not
Itself a thought but rather an awareness
Already and innately thought-free.

The challenge of meditation then, is not
The one that was formulated by the Zen Master
Dogen: "How to think 'not thinking'?"

Instead the challenge
Of meditation is to think in a
Truly meditative way – to be *aware* of
The thoughts that arise in us and to
Be the thought-free Awareness
Of those thoughts.

Awareness as Freedom

The Awareness of a thing
Is not itself a thing,
It is a thing-free Awareness.

The Awareness of a thought
Is not itself a thought.
It is a thought-free Awareness.

The Awareness of an emotion
Is not itself an emotion.
It is an emotion-free Awareness.

The Awareness of a sensation
Is not itself a sensation.
It is a sensation-free Awareness.

The awareness of an
Inner impulse to act or speak
Is not itself an impulse to act or speak.
Being free of impulses to act or speak,
Awareness is what allows us
To act and speak freely.

Remember, then, always and forever,
At each and every moment of your life,
At all times and in all situations, that
Awareness alone is Freedom.

Awareness as Body and Soul

How do you know you have a body?
Because it is something you carry about with you?
Because you can look at it in the mirror and see it?
Because it can be seen and touched by others - or
Because you feel it from within, from out of an
Inner, feeling Awareness of your body?

The 'soul' IS the body,
Not the body as perceived from without
But the body as you are aware of it,
As you feel it - from within.

Yet this inner, feeling
Awareness of your body does
Not end at its outer boundary or skin.
For your body itself IS an awareness -
An awareness of every other body
Around it in space - and of
Everything going on
In your life and in
The world.

That is why you

Are as much aware of your

Self as a whole - your 'soul' - as

You are aware, not just of your body as a whole

From top to bottom, head to toe, but also

'Every body' in the world around you.

Whether thing or person,

Here or there.

The pure Awareness of your body,

That which allows you to feel it from within

Is not itself anything bodily, and yet it is the Universal

Soul of all things – that Divine Soul which embodies

Itself as *every* body, and pervades the spaces

Within and around them.

Awareness of self

Is an awareness of the body, felt as

A body OF awareness or 'soul', one made up

Not of flesh and bone, but of felt

Tones, qualities and textures *of*

Awareness itself.

For what body is it

That can feel lighter or heavier?

Smaller or bigger, irrespective

Of it weight and size.

What body is it that can feel
More or less airy, fiery, fluid or solid.
Closed off in yourself or open to the world,
'Closer' or more 'distant' to others, 'warmer' or
'Cooler' towards them - yet all this irrespective
Of your 'physical' temperature,
Shape, density or distance?

What body is it that can 'touch' or
Feel 'touched' by others, 'move or be 'moved' by them,
Yet without any physical contact or movement at all?
It is your immortal body of awareness or soul.

Awareness as all the Elements

Why do somebody's eyes shine brightly?
Because of the light reflected off their surface, or
Because of the luminous intensity of Awareness
That shines through their gaze?

Light is a manifestation of the Light of Awareness.
Fire is a manifestation of the ever- and all-transforming
Fire of Awareness.

Air is a manifestation of
The all-pervasive Aether and
Breath of Awareness.

Water is a manifestation of
The Fluidity of Awareness.

Earth is a manifestation of
Its solidity and fertility.

Awareness matters, because
Matter is a materialisation of Awareness.
Just as 'energy' is the formative activity of Awareness.
Just as space is a vast universal field of Awareness, and
Time is the presencing of things in that field, so
All bodies are Embodiments of Awareness,
Formed of its Elemental qualities.

Just as pure Awareness
Can be breathed as blessed air,
So it can also be sensed as flowing,
Fluid warmth, a radiant light, an intense
Fire, a myriad of sparkling colours, or
A symphony of silent sounds.

Awareness as Awakening

There is all that occurs in our dreams,
And there is the Awareness from and within which
Our dreams emerge and take shape.

There is the dreamt self,
The self we experience in our dreams,
And there is the dreaming self - the Awareness
That dreams us and all that we dream.

Likewise, there is all that we
Experience or 'dream' as our waking lives, and
There is the Awareness within and out of which
All waking events and experiences arise.

Space is not 'caused' by any thing within it,
Dreaming is not 'caused' or enclosed by anything we dream.
Awareness is not 'caused' or enclosed by any thing we are aware of.
True 'enlightenment' is awakening to The Awareness
That dreams us and all that we experience -
Whether asleep or awake.

Awareness is the source of
'The Dreaming' by which all things arise, and
Through which they are dreamt and materialised.
Be Aware of all things then, as Dreamings of Awareness.

Yet do not lose yourself in those Dreamings, but
Awaken to the Awareness that is their source -
The Divine Dreaming Awareness.

There are many who know what it is like
To wake up not 'from' but within a dream;
To become Aware that they are dreaming and,
Through this very Awareness, to act with greater
Freedom and Awareness within the dream.
This is called 'lucid dreaming'.

The Practice of Awareness
Is a practice of 'lucid waking',
Enabling us to wake up within the dream that
Is our everyday waking life.

How? By Awakening to
The pure Awareness of whatever we are experiencing,
Rather than identifying with any elements of that
Experiencing - positive or negative,
Pleasurable or painful.
Bodily or mental.

.

Awareness as the Self

Who are you?

You are not what you think.

You are not what you feel you are.

You are not your experience of yourself.

You are not your experience of the world.

You are more than the sum of all your experiences.

You are The Awareness of all you experience within and around you.

Yet that Awareness is not 'yours' or 'mine' but the essence of The Divine.

It is not an Awareness encapsulated in space or time, and

Nor is it a function or product of your body or mind.

Instead you, your body, your mind, and every

Single thing and being you are aware of,

Is a shape taken by that Awareness,

Within that Awareness.

Within God.

Awareness as God and as all the gods

'God' does not 'have' but IS Awareness,
Not an awareness that is 'yours' or 'mine', but
One which is absolute, unbounded, universal and Divine.
To recognise 'God' in all things is to recognise Awareness in all things.
God is everything and more because Awareness is everything and more.
There is nothing outside God, as there is nothing outside Awareness.
Awareness is everything, just as everything in turn IS an Awareness -
A unique, individualised portion and expression of that
Divine-Universal Awareness which IS God.

Since everything is a part of
The Divine Universal Awareness as a whole
As a whole, INSEPARABLE from its entirety,
Every thing and each of us IS that whole -
Everything and each of us IS God.

Yet since everything is also a DISTINCT
Part of the Divine-Universal Awareness as a whole,
A unique expression of it - so also is everything
And each of us 'a god'.

God and 'the gods'
Are distinct yet inseparable,
For each being is both an inseparable portion of the
Whole that is God - and thus God - and a unique
Expression of it – and thus 'a god'.

Behind all things are the unique
Pattern, shapes, qualities and textures of
The Divine-Universal Awareness itself,
Of 'God', that endow them with
Godhood, making them into
Gods in themselves.

INTRODUCTION

Welcome to the World of Awareness

Welcome to the 'pure land' of knowledge, a land of 'pure knowledge'. This 'pure knowledge' is not knowledge 'of' or 'about' things but direct subjective knowing. Though it has had many names - gnosis, wisdom, intuition, realization, enlightenment, awakening - its essence, quite simply, is *awareness*. Welcome then, to the World of Awareness. Welcome too, to 'The Awareness Principle' - a principle transcending both science and religion as we know them. The Awareness Principle transcends science because it recognises that the fundamental scientific fact and the true starting point of all scientific investigation is not the existence of a universe of things or beings in space and time but *awareness* of such a universe. By this I mean not simply my or your awareness, or even our awareness or God's awareness but awareness as such. The single most important misconception running through the entire history of Western thought is the belief that awareness is either a mere by-product of matter or the private property of individual beings. What if it is the other way round? What if all things and all beings are but individualised portions and expressions of an ultimate or absolute awareness - one that is not the product or property of any thing or being we are aware of? From this point of view 'God' too, is not some sort of supreme being with awareness. Instead God *is* awareness – a divine and all-pervasive awareness of which all beings and all things are but a portion and expression.

Theists and atheists can argue endlessly about whether God 'exists' without ever asking what we mean by the word 'God'. What neither of them question is whether or not what we call 'God' is any type of existing being at all. There is a paradox here. Let us consider it more deeply. The paradox is that the 'existence' of God would reduce what we call 'God' to one existing thing or being among others, thus turning God into something limited and finite –

hardly a fitting understanding of the divine. What I call 'The Awareness Principle' transcends the question of God's existence or non-existence - arguing that even though not an existing thing or being like any other, God is nevertheless the ultimate *reality* behind and within all things and all beings. That is because before and behind all existence – all existing things and beings – is *awareness* – awareness of existence and awareness of being. Let us consider this again. To ask whether God exists is like asking whether you or I exist – whether we *are*? How do we know that we exist – that we *are*? How do you know that you exist – that you *are*? How do any of us know that we exist – that we are? We know because each of us is *aware* of being. It is this most intimate, profound and primordial *awareness* of being that belongs to the very core and essence of every existing being. Since this basic *awareness* of being belongs to the very core of every existing being it also transcends every existing being. This pure and profound awareness of being, and not any thing or being we are aware of, is the true essence and reality of God – the divine.

Whilst God is not some supreme Creator being 'with' awareness, God *is* that awareness which is the absolute, universal and divine reality behind and within all Creation and all Creatures. People who believe that God is a supreme being however, and not a supreme and absolute awareness, are forced to believe that God 'made' or 'created' the world out of nothing. Atheistic scientists, on the other hand, still seek an alternative explanation of how the universe and all things came to be. For Creationists the answer to the question of how things came to be is some Big Being they call God. For scientists it is some cosmic event they call the Big Bang. Both are badly mistaken. A theist is someone who believes that God is an existing being that has or possesses an omniscient awareness. An atheist denies the existence of such a being. Modern science claims that awareness can be reduced to the by-product, property or function of some existing thing, like the human brain. What they are actually claiming is that awareness can be reduced to or explained by some particular thing we are aware *of*. Yet there is another paradox here to consider more deeply. For surely just to be aware of something, to perceive it and be capable of observing and studying it, already assumes the *reality* of awareness as such? Thus to seek a cause for awareness in any thing we are aware *of* – the brain for example - is like seeking a cause for a dream, or for the whole experience of dreaming as such, in one particular thing we dream of. This is patent absurdity. But it is an absurdity that has yet to be clearly pointed out. The Awareness Principle does so. For its 1st Principle of Awareness is simply that Awareness as such *is* the 1st Principle of all things. Why? Because awareness cannot – *in principle* – be explained by or reduced to any thing or being we are aware *of*. That is why I prefer to use the term 'awareness' rather than 'consciousness'. Consciousness is awareness *of* something. Awareness on the other hand is consciousness *as such* – pure consciousness.

This is not just a philosophical or semantic difference. The things you are conscious or aware *of* may include your reflections on or 'felt sense' of the words you have been reading, bodily sensations or needs such as hunger or thirst, your thoughts and feelings, the basic mood or 'tone' of feeling you find yourself in, your perceptions of the room around you and the objects within it, things that are concerning you or challenges that you face in your current life, memories of the past or anticipations of the future etc. You may be conscious or aware *of* any or all of such things. Yet *the awareness as such* is not any of those things. To understand this, just think of the space you are sitting in and the objects in it. The space contains your body and those objects but *is not itself* a body or object. Similarly, the awareness of a need, desire, sensation or impulse, feeling or thought *is not itself* a need or desire, sensation or impulse, feeling or thought.

This principle is one of the most important Principles of Awareness that leads us to what I call The Practice of Awareness. Let us take one example. The awareness of a thought is not itself a thought. Therefore it is something innately free of thought. Often when people talk about meditation, particularly Buddhist sitting meditation or Zen, they are caught up in the idea that to meditate properly and achieve a higher, more 'enlightened' state of awareness they must *stop thinking*. Even the Zen masters thought so. The Japanese master Dogen said that Zen is all about finding the answer to a single question. The question as he put it was "How do you think 'not thinking'?" The answer to it is simpler than most people imagine – namely that there is no need in the first place to 'think' not-thinking. All we need to 'do' is to simply be *aware* of our thoughts. For though thoughts and thinking occur within awareness, the awareness of them is not itself a thought or thought process. The true question is not "How to think 'not thinking'".

The true question is how not to *think* thinking but how to simply be aware of our thoughts and thinking, knowing that awareness of our thoughts and our thinking is something innately and entirely free of thoughts and thinking. Likewise, our awareness of a desire is not itself a desire and thus something innately free of desire. Thus there is no need to suppress any desires to be free of them. Let me say that again, there is no need to stop thinking - or to stop having needs, impulses and desires, in order to be free of them – for awareness as such is innately free of any thing we are aware of - whether a need, impulse, desire, feeling or thought.

I define The Awareness Principle as a new foundational principle for science, philosophy, psychology, religion and life. It is a new foundational principle for *science* because it recognises that the starting point of scientific investigation – the most fundamental scientific 'fact' - is *not* the 'objective' existence of a world of bodies in space and time but subjective *awareness* of such a universe. It is a new foundational principle of philosophy because it recognises that *awareness* of existence or being is prior to and therefore transcends all existing things - all 'beings'. It is a new foundational principle of psychology because it argues how, in principle, awareness cannot be either the by-product of any thing we are aware of, or the private property of any self or being we are aware of. It is a new foundational principle of religion because it allows us to recognise that God indeed does not 'exist' as a supreme being with awareness, but *is* awareness - and therefore the ultimate reality behind all things. Thus just as there can, in principle, be nothing 'outside' of space or 'before' time (the problem of Big Bang theory) so there can - in principle - be nothing outside awareness, nothing outside God.

Finally, The Awareness Principle is a new principle of life. For the basic Principle of Awareness leads to a new type of 'yoga' or Practice of Awareness – one which liberates our consciousness from attachment to any thing we are aware of. It does so not simply by repetitious talk of 'non-attachment' or 'mindfulness', as if these words were mantras - but instead by clearly explaining and re-minding us of a basic and fundamental principle: namely that the *awareness* of a need, impulse, desire, feeling or thought is not itself a need, impulse, desire, feeling or thought, and is therefore innately or inherently free of any thing we are aware of. The awareness of any thing is not itself any thing at all. Yet the fact that awareness is 'no-thing' does not mean that it is *nothing*. On the contrary, it is what makes awareness more real than anything. Awareness, then, is not anything. And yet, awareness, ultimately, is everything. For there is nothing – no thing – that is not a shape taken by awareness, a manifestation of awareness and an individualised portion of that ultimate all-pervasive awareness that is God.

Put simply, the Awareness Principle recognises, in principle, three fundamental truths. The *first* fundamental truth is that awareness as such is no 'thing' – and cannot be reduced to any thing we are aware of. The second fundamental truth is that *awareness is everything*. The third, no less fundamental truth, is that *everything is an awareness*. A thought or feeling for example, is not just some thing we are aware of. It in turn is an awareness of something else. We take it for granted of course, that human beings are not just 'things' we happen to be aware of. Instead we understand that each human being is themselves an *aware* being. That is not to say that human beings - or any beings - simply have or possess awareness. Rather, like every atom or cell, animal or plant, rock or tree, every human being *is* an awareness. That is not to say that atomic, molecular or cellular awareness has the same character as human awareness. Yet the human body is an organic symphony of the awareness that constitutes each of its atom and molecules, cells and organs. And the human being is a unique and ever-changing constellation of different tones and textures, movements and directions, patterns and qualities of awareness.

To truly be aware of another human being is to sense the unique tones and qualities of awareness which shape and colour *their* experience of the world and other people. When we speak of another human being as 'warm' or 'cool', 'close' or 'distant', 'closed' or 'open', 'light' or 'heavy', 'bright' or 'dull', 'rigid' or 'flexible', 'solid' or 'airy', 'icy' or 'fiery' we are not merely describing them in 'metaphorical' terms - describing our sense of a person's 'soul' with words deriving from sensory qualities of things. Instead we are giving expression to innate sensual qualities of their awareness or 'soul' - and of awareness or 'soul' as such. It is not that sensory qualities of things become mere metaphors for soul qualities. Rather it is these very sensual qualities of awareness or soul – soul qualities - that find *expression* in the sensory qualities of all things. 'The World of Awareness' *is* the 'soul world' lying behind and beyond our physical world and life. There, as in our dreams, the qualities of awareness or soul qualities that colour our moods and come to expression as sensory phenomena and their qualities – a dark or black mood being perceived as a dark or black cloud for example. Similarly a euphoric feeling of 'levity' or being 'uplifted' may translate itself into a dream of our body levitating or flying. What we experience as our *dream body* is nothing but our eternal *soul body* as such. This is not our objective physical body – our body as perceived from without, but our body as we are aware of it and feel it from within - our inwardly felt or 'subjective' body. What we call 'the soul' *is* our inwardly felt body – essentially a body of *awareness* made up of sensual shapes, tones and textures *of* awareness.

Our most direct and immediate inner awareness of our bodies is imbued with tangible 'elemental' qualities - ranging from dense solidity or rigidity to watery fluidity, airy diffuseness, spacious expansiveness or fiery vitality. It is such 'elemental' soul qualities that the sages of the past knew as the true meaning of 'the five elements' – understanding them as both basic elements of nature and our own human soul nature. Elemental qualities of awareness find expression not only in our immediate proprioceptive awareness of our own bodies but constitute the 'soul' of all bodies – no matter whether these be dreamt or physical, bodies of people or bodies of seemingly inanimate, insentient or unaware 'things'. Our physical bodies themselves are but patterns of atomic, molecular and cellular awareness. Though their human physical *form* may decompose when we die, the awareness that imbues every atom of them does not. The individual combinations of soul qualities that shape our sense of *self* and imbue our body with its unique *form* survive after death in the form of the 'soul body' itself. This remains perceptible in the soul world – the world of awareness - even without physical form. Each night it takes non-physical form in our dreams - not only in the form of our dreamt body as such, but as the entire 'body' of our dream environment and every other body within it. Just as our entire dream environment is the larger *body* of our dreaming awareness, so is our entire waking world the larger body of our waking awareness - itself part of a multidimensional World of Awareness that we remain largely *asleep* to.

The Awareness Principle Defined

The Awareness Principle is a radical new foundational principle for life, science and religion. In contrast to the current basis of most scientific, spiritual and religious thinking it is based on the recognition that Awareness alone is - in Principle - the sole possible reality underlying and constituting all things and all beings.

The Awareness Principle is thus also all of the following:

- **The sole possible 'Theory of Everything'.**

- **The most revolutionary new philosophy of religion, science and everyday life.**

- **The simplest, most practical principle by which to transform your life and transform our world.**

- **The most radical re-interpretation of the fundamental nature of 'God' and 'Spirit', 'Matter' and 'Energy', 'Space' and 'Time', 'Creation' and 'Evolution', 'Being' and 'Consciousness', 'Soul' and 'Body', 'Life' and 'Death', 'Freedom' and 'Enlightenment'.**

Beyond Science, Psychology and Religion

The Awareness Principle transcends Science, Psychology and Religion as we know them - offering in their place a new foundational principle for both knowledge and life.

- **The Awareness Principle transcends 'science' as we know it, because it recognises that the most basic scientific 'fact' or 'reality' is not the existence of a universe of matter, energy and space-time but *awareness* of such a universe.**

- **The Awareness Principle transcends 'psychology' as we know it, because it recognises that awareness is universal and all-pervasive in character – not a purely personal and privately owned 'soul' or 'psyche' that is bounded by our bodies or a product of our brains.**

- **The Awareness Principle transcends 'religion' as we know it, because it recognises that 'God' is not a supreme being that has or 'possesses' awareness but *is* awareness - a universal awareness of which all individual bodies, beings or 'souls' are a unique portion and expression.**

Historical Roots of The Awareness Principle

The Awareness Principle has its historic roots in both the European philosophical tradition known as 'Phenomenology' and Indian 'Advaita' philosophy. Both recognised in principle that 'transcendental subjectivity' or 'pure awareness' – awareness *as such* - is the ultimate reality behind all things and thus also the foundation of all true thinking. Yet whereas European phenomenology offered only forms of abstract reflection on or about pure awareness, Advaita offered a yogic path of total identification with it, and through this a direct spiritual experience of awareness as both transcendent and immanent in all things.

In particular, it was in the metaphysical theology of 'Shaivist Advaita' or 'Kashmir Shaivism' that awareness was acknowledged as the godhead itself under the name of the absolute or unsurpassable reality ('Anuttara') lying behind and pervading all things, and personified by the god Shiva. This philosophy came to its most consummate and refined experiential and conceptual expression through the work of the great 10th century tantric metaphysician and yogin – Acharya Abhinavagupta.

'The Awareness Principle' is an attempt to newly conceptualise and crystallise the essence of this metaphysical tradition in the most concise, logically consistent and clear cut way possible. In doing so I make frequent use of the traditional form of treatises or 'Tantras', each of which consists of a series of condensed metaphysical propositions ('Karikas') whose individual threads ('Sutras') interweave to constitute a singular logical and metaphysical 'loom' ('Tantra').

Opposed to today's global 'monotheism of money' (Marx) stands an ancient monism of a singular awareness – that unbounded, universal or divine awareness that is manifest in all things. The Awareness Principle reargues and rearticulates this multi-dimensional monism of awareness. It reasserts the basic principle that God is Awareness, that there can be nothing 'outside' awareness as there can be nothing outside space - and that therefore awareness – God – is all there is.

Historically, the Awareness Principle follows the metaphysics of the medieval Hindu Tantras in understanding space itself as identical with pure awareness - both inseparable and absolutely distinct from anything that exists within it. Buddhist metaphysics on the other hand, takes 'space' *merely* as 'emptiness' and denies inherent reality, existence or 'being' to every thing within it. The Awareness Principle stands in contrast to what might be termed 'The Being Principle' of Western metaphysics – which elevates Existence or Being to the status of supreme principle, and identifies God either with Being as such or with a Supreme Being. In place of 'The Being Principle' however, Buddhism puts forward a principle of 'Non-Being' - asserting the inherent emptiness of all existence, and turning 'Emptiness' itself into an Absolute, rather than its divine essence – Awareness.

THE PRINCIPLE AND PRACTICE OF AWARENESS

The Principle of Awareness

There is the way we are feeling.

There is the way we think about it.

There is the way we express our thoughts and feelings.

There is the way they colour our view of the world.

There is the way they influence how we see others.

There is the way they shape our sense of ourselves.

There is the way they lead us to behave.

There is the way they affect our bodies.

And there is **Awareness** ...

Awareness of our thoughts and feelings.

Awareness of the way we express them.

Awareness of the way they affect our bodies and behaviour.

Awareness of how they lead us to act and react to others.

Awareness of the way they colour our view of the world.

Awareness of the way they affect our sense of ourselves.

This awareness of our feelings and thoughts is not itself a feeling or thought.

This awareness of our bodies and minds is not itself anything bodily or mental.

This awareness, like space, embraces and transcends each and every thing we are aware of within it.

This, in a nutshell, is **The Awareness Principle**.

The Primary Distinction and the Primary Choice

Think of all you are experiencing at any point in time - whether inwardly or outwardly, physically or emotionally - together with all your mental reflections on your experience – as one side of a coin or line. Think of the other side of the coin or line as nothing but the very awareness of experiencing it. The two sides of that coin or line are inseparable – and yet they are also absolutely distinct.

The Awareness Principle is based on this *primary distinction* - drawing a line between anything we *experience* and the pure *awareness* of experiencing it.

things we experience

---

the awareness of experiencing those things

The Practice of Awareness is a *primary choice* based on this primary distinction. It is the choice to identify with the pure awareness of the things we experience rather than identifying with those things themselves. By 'things we experience' I mean anything from an outwardly experienced object, situation, event or action, to an inwardly experienced impulse, sensation, mood, emotion, memory, anticipation or thought.

In writings on Eastern spiritual teachings too much mystery is usually made of the idea of a 'pure' or 'transcendental' awareness that is free of thoughts, emotions, drives and desires etc. and the 'effort' needed to attain this awareness. In reality, if The Awareness Principle is understood, no great effort at all is required to attain this state of pure or 'transcendental' awareness. The awareness of a physical object such as a leather chair is not itself a chair and nor is that awareness made of leather. Neither is the *awareness* of a thought itself a thought. Similarly, the awareness of any 'thing' (whether an object, situation, event, mood, emotion, desire, impulse, action, thought etc.) is *not itself* a 'thing' or 'thought' of any sort. The 'awareness principle' is simply the recognition that *awareness - in principle* – is innately 'pure', both thought-free and 'thing-free' in general. It does not need to be effortfully 'emptied' of any thoughts or things to be *made* 'pure'. For just as space is absolutely distinct from all the objects within it, so also is awareness as such absolutely distinct from all its contents – from all we are aware *of*. It does not need to be 'emptied' of all content to be as clear and pure as the 'empty' space around objects.

A Basic Practice of Awareness: Whether sitting, standing or lying, and without closing your eyes, simply be aware of the different things you are currently experiencing – things of any and all sorts, from physical objects and sensations to emotions, actions and thoughts. Now simply become more aware of the clear space around your body, and around all the physical objects in your environment. Feel a similar clear space around any 'things' you are experiencing inside you, such as emotions and thoughts. In this way you will come to *experience* the clear space-like quality of pure awareness as such, and be able to identify with it rather than anything in it.

All the Practices of Awareness, evolved from The Awareness Principle, that make up 'The New Yoga of Awareness' are based on passing from a *new awareness of experience* to a *new experience of awareness* – whether as the clearness of space ('Kha'), as the translucent light of awareness (Prakasha), and as its vitalising aetheric air or breath (Akasha/Prana).

Sitting comfortably, take five minutes to be aware of what you are currently experiencing within you. Note down on paper or make a mental note of the different elements of your experiencing, distinguishing them into three categories as below.

PHYSICAL SENSATIONS	EMOTIONAL FEELINGS	THOUGHTS AND QUESTIONS
e.g. a fluttering sensation in my stomach	e.g. feeling 'anxious'	e.g. how can I best say what I need to say to person X?

Emotional terms like 'anxious', 'upset', 'depressed' etc. are actually just umbrella labels for a huge variety of possible physical sensations, states and feelings. Concentrate on your direct bodily experience of your physical states and sensations, not on the emotion labels. If your thoughts take the form 'I am anxious' or 'I feel depressed', dismiss the words and ask yourself what exactly it is you are anxious, angry or depressed about. If you don't know, staying with your awareness to the specific physical sensation of the 'anxiety', 'anger' or 'depression' will eventually tell you. By staying with the physical sensation of your emotional feelings, ways of expressing them will come to mind that don't require you to use label-words like 'anxiety'. Instead they will have more to do with what lies underneath your feelings – what they themselves may be seeking to make you more aware of.

Identifying with this transcendental awareness by identifying with and breathing the pure translucency of space itself is **The Practice of Awareness** in its essence. This practice frees us from identification with our bodies and minds, with our feelings and thoughts, sensations and perceptions, actions and reactions, behaviours and beliefs – with anything we are or can be aware of. At the same time it creates space for us to become aware of far more dimensions of reality, for new, clearer feelings and thoughts to arise - and with them a new sense of ourselves. In particular it allows us to identify with that Self that is not simply aware of this or that but IS awareness – pure and simple. Not 'my' or 'your' awareness, but that absolute or Divine Awareness which is present within us all as our divine Awareness Self.

Attaining Freedom through Awareness

The Awareness Principle and the Practice of Awareness are about how the power of awareness can transform our consciousness and free our everyday lives from all that is a source of dis-ease for us.

If people get lost in watching TV or playing computer games, in work or domestic chores, in thinking or talking, in worrying about life or in feeling particular emotions, pains - or even pleasures - then they may be 'conscious' but they are not aware.

Whenever our consciousness becomes overly focussed or fixated on any one thing we are conscious of, dominated by it or identified with it, we lose awareness.

For unlike ordinary 'consciousness', awareness is not focussed on any one thing we experience. Awareness is more like the space surrounding us and surrounding all things we are aware of. For space is not the same as any 'thing' within it.

Living with and within awareness is like truly living with and within space – which both encompasses but is also absolutely distinct from each and every thing within it.

To transform our ordinary consciousness into awareness therefore, means first of all becoming more aware of space itself – both the outer space around us and surrounding things, and also the inner space surrounding our thoughts, feelings, impulses and sensations.

Enhancing our bodily awareness of the space around us is the first step to helping us to experience space itself – outer and inner – as an expansive spacious field of awareness – a field free of domination by anything we may be conscious of or experience within it.

'Achieving freedom through awareness' therefore means transforming our ordinary consciousness or 'focal awareness' into a new type of spacious 'field awareness' – for this is the true and literal meaning of 'expanding' our consciousness.

If we are able to sense and identify with the spacious awareness field around and within us, then we can do two things. We can both freely acknowledge and affirm everything we experience or are conscious of within that field – whether pleasant or unpleasant. And yet at the same time we can stop our 'consciousness' getting sucked into, stuck on, focussed or fixated on any one thing.

The capacity to constantly come back to the spacious awareness field frees us from all the things our consciousness normally gets so fixated on that we can no longer distinguish or free ourselves from them. True freedom is freedom from identification with anything we experience – anything we are 'conscious' or 'aware' *of*. This freedom comes from sensing and identifying with that spacious awareness field within which we experience all things, outwardly and inwardly.

Awareness is not the same as what is often called 'mindfulness' – for it includes awareness of all we experience as mind or mental activity.

An old spiritual tradition has it that awareness itself is 'God' – understood as an infinitely spacious field of consciousness. This tradition also understood awareness as the source of all beings and as the eternal core or essence of our being – as our higher self. Just as through enhanced awareness of space we can experience it as a boundlessly expansive awareness field, so can we also experience our own spiritual core or essence as a powerful centre of awareness within that field.

Most forms of therapy or counselling are limited by the fact that they do not distinguish 'consciousness' or 'focal awareness' from field awareness. They themselves focus the client's consciousness on its contents – on things they are conscious or unconscious of – rather than transforming that focal consciousness into a clear and spacious awareness field - and centring the client's awareness in that field.

Both the Awareness Principle and the Practice of Awareness are founded on a fundamental distinction between consciousness and awareness, between any thing we are consciously experiencing on the one hand, and the pure awareness of experiencing it on the other. Identifying this pure awareness with space is the most effective way of experiencing it.

This fundamental distinction offers us in turn a fundamental choice – either to identify ourselves with things we are conscious of, or to identify instead with the very awareness of them – an awareness that will automatically free our consciousness from domination by any of its contents, anything we experience.

An important help in making this choice is to remind yourself of a simple truth: that just as awareness of an object is not itself an object, so is awareness of a thought, emotion or physical sensation not itself a thought, emotion or sensation. Awareness of any thoughts you have is something innately thought-free – just as awareness of any impulses, emotions and sensations you feel is something innately free of those impulses, emotions or sensations. Awareness is Freedom.

Living without - and with - Awareness

LIVING WITHOUT AWARENESS

A man wakes up in the morning. He feels grumpy and annoyed. The first thing that comes into his mind are feelings left over from what his partner has said on the previous evening, words that annoyed and left him feeling hurt.

He turns the conversation over and over in his head while he prepares to go to work. The more he thinks about it the angrier he gets, feeling not only justifiably 'hurt' but hateful in a way he dare not express.

He wants to find a way of putting his feelings of hurt and anger out of his mind and stop thinking about them, yet at the same time feels an impulse to let them out on his partner in an explosive and hateful way.

Caught in this dilemma, he thinks, how can he possibly concentrate on work feeling all this?

Identifying with this thought he does indeed end up being unconcentrated, closed off and distracted all day, with no resolution of his feelings in sight.

When he comes home and sees his partner again he is still torn between repressing his feelings and expressing them in a vengeful way.

He feels even angrier towards her as a result of feeling himself in this conflicted state, seeing it too, as her fault.

LIVING WITH AWARENESS

A man wakes up in the morning. He feels grumpy and annoyed. The first thing that comes into his mind is the row he had with his partner on the previous evening, the words that annoyed him and left him feeling hurt.

This time he is more aware however. Instead of just letting his mind run on, so fixated on his feelings and identified with them that they get stronger in a way he 'knows' will ruin his day - he practices awareness.

First he says to himself 'It is not that I AM grumpy, annoyed or hurt'. "I am simply AWARE of feelings of 'grumpiness', 'annoyance' and 'hurt'. I AM AWARE also, that the more I focus on them the stronger these feelings become, and I am aware too of the THOUGHT – not the 'fact' – that this will 'ruin my day.'"

Then he takes a second major step. Instead of identifying with these feelings and this thought he chooses to identify with the simple AWARENESS of them.

He does so first by reminding himself that the AWARENESS of any thought or emotion is not itself a thought or emotion. Instead it is more like a free and empty space in which all thoughts and feelings can be held and affirmed - yet without becoming filled, dominated and preoccupied by them.

As a result, his feelings spiral even more in intensity and at the same time he tries to reign them inside his body, contracting the space he feels inside his body and making him feel even more explosive.

She in turn picks up his reigned-in emotions and bodily tenseness and finally unable to bear or contain the tensions herself says something that bursts the bubble, letting him explode in anger.

The result is that she now feels angry and hurt, and (another) mighty row results.

The row itself does not resolve anything or lead to knew and helpful insights that raise their awareness of important aspects of themselves and their relationship.

Instead it just leaves them temporarily relieved or emptied of their feelings - whilst at the same time still harbouring the same thoughts and judgements towards one another, regarding each other as the 'cause' of their own thoughts and feelings, and identifying with these feelings and thoughts towards one another.

The next day ends up being no better for either, with both feeling isolated in themselves.

Not able to identify with and feel themselves in a space of awareness big enough to make room for their own feelings - let alone those of their partner – they remain preoccupied with themselves and able to 'contain' their feelings only by contracting and withdrawing into their own separate and isolating spaces.

He succeeds in identifying with AWARENESS by becoming deliberately more aware of the actual space around his body, sensing it as a larger, unfilled space around and between his thoughts and feelings too.

As a result of putting himself in this more expansive space, he no longer feels a need to close off, tense and tighten his body in order to prevent himself exploding with the feelings and thoughts that filled it. For he knows that this tightening is exactly what contracts his inner space and makes it feel so full.

He no longer feels himself 'in a space' that is so contracted, crammed and preoccupied by his initial thoughts and feelings, that it leaves no free space of awareness for other important things like his work, and no space too for new insights to arise into the feelings that might have been behind his partner's 'hurtful' words. Such insights do indeed come to him spontaneously in the intervals of his work, and at the end of an undistracted working day.

Still identifying with his sense of being in a space 'big' enough to contain both his own feelings and those of his partner, he is able to not only calmly communicate his feelings but also share his empathic understanding of the feelings that might have been behind the words that 'hurt' him. The result is a hostility-free dialogue which makes them both feel better and more 'together' – feeling once again that they dwell in a shared space of togetherness.

The Awareness Principle Again

AWARENESS cannot be explained by and is not caused by any thing or thought, sensation or emotion, conception or perception, image or symbol, for it is the very *condition* for our experience of any thing or thought, sensation or emotion, conception or perception, image or symbol whatsoever.

AWARENESS of any thing or thought, sensation or emotion, conception or perception, image or symbol, *is not itself* a thing or thought, sensation or emotion, conception or perception, image or symbol.

AWARENESS is thing-free and thought-free, free of sensations and emotions, conceptions and perceptions, images and symbols. Awareness is Freedom itself – the freedom to affirm all that you are aware of, without becoming bound to it.

AWARENESS is also the creative source and inexhaustible womb of ever-new things and thoughts, ever-new sensations and emotions, images and symbols, conceptions and perceptions – the womb of ever-new worlds. It is also the wordless source of all true words – "the wordless knowledge within the word".

AWARENESS has its own innately *sensual* qualities and its own innate *bodily* shapes, tones and textures. Conversely, our body is no mere object or thing but an immediately experienced tone and texture *of* awareness. If people are deluded into thinking of the body only as the biological basis of their 'awareness' or 'consciousness' it tends to disappear from their awareness – and is no longer experienced as a sensuous shape, tone and texture *of* awareness.

Awareness beyond Identity - the 'Atman'

Every aspect of our experiencing is tinged with that specific sense of self or 'personal identity' by which we know ourselves in a given life, and which we associate with our given name. Our every experience of something or someone 'other than self' – whether a thing or person – is inseparable from a particular experience of ourselves – indeed it makes up our experience of self. Thus everything experienced by an individual named 'X' - 'Mary Wilson' for example - is coloured through and through with what might be called 'Mary Wilson-ness'. Conversely, it is what colours Mary Wilson's whole self-experience – her experience of 'Being Mary Wilson'. Personal identity then, belongs to the realm of *experiencing* – not the *awareness* of all we experience, including the experience of self. For our experienced sense of self or personal identity is but a part of our experiencing as a whole.

This understanding however, demands that the idea of 'self-awareness' be subjected to closer examination. For if 'self-awareness' is taken to mean 'awareness of self', then this very 'awareness' cannot, in principle, be the property or activity of whatever 'self' *there is an awareness of.* Awareness of self, in principle, transcends any self we experience or are aware of. No self *can be aware of itself.* There can only be *an awareness of that self.* This awareness must by nature transcend that self – and any experienced self. For no *experienced* self then, can be the *experiencer* of itself.

Recognising that the experienced self is something in constant flux and not a fixed identity, many Buddhist thinkers negated the Hindu notion of a higher or divine self (the 'Atman') and argued that there was no 'self' behind our experience. Yet in the first *sutra* of the treatise or *tantra* known as the *Shiva Sutras* the Buddhist notion of 'no-self' ('Anatman') was itself overcome through a new concept of the Atman, understanding it not as any *experienced* self, but as the *experiencing* self – not as any self that 'has' or 'possesses' awareness (even a so-called 'witnessing' self) but as that self which *is* awareness ('Chaitanyatman'). This 'awareness self' transcends personal identity – in particular the sense of self or identity associated with the limited self or 'Jiva'. Instead, being identical with awareness as such, it is also identical with the universal and divine awareness known under the god-name of 'Shiva'.

The awareness of a particular identity is like the awareness of acting and experiencing a role or part in a drama. That *awareness* does not itself *belong* to the role or part being acted and experienced. It does not even belong to the 'actor' acting the part – for even the actor's off-stage identity is itself a collection of parts being acted and experienced. The distinction central to The Awareness Principle – between all that we experience and the pure awareness of experiencing it – therefore also applies to the 'self' as we experience it in a given life. By recognising that each and every aspect of our experience in this life is bound up with the particular sense of personal identity – the one associated with our name and present-life identity – we can learn to transcend that identity, and discover instead that eternal Self known as the *Atman*. For this is a Self which, being nothing but awareness as such, transcends this and all our lives and identities.

In order to transform the many meditational Practices of Awareness that follow from The Awareness Principle into a direct realisation of that Self which *is* Awareness, it can be helpful to read the text below – filling in the gaps in the text by mentally reading and speaking *your own full name*:

The ………… Identity:

I 'am' …………

Because this 'I' is one identified ('I'-dentified) with my immediate experiencing,

because every element and aspect of my experiencing is tinged with

'…………-ness'

and because my every thought and feeling, impulse and action, is something

bound up with my entire present-life identity *as* ………..

Yet whilst everything 'I' experience and do is bound up with the ………..

identity

the pure *awareness* of that experience and identity *transcends* that experience and

identity.

I *am*………… only because I *am not* ………..

Instead, I am the *awareness* of 'being' …………

This awareness of 'being' ………… transcends my ………… identity and all

my identities, both in this life and in others.

It alone is my prime, divine and eternal identity – the *Atman*.

The Basic Practice of Awareness (1)

1. Without closing your eyes, take time to be aware of all there is to be aware of both within and around you – impulses, sensations, emotions and thoughts within you; the air, light, objects and space around you.

2. Attend particularly to your wordless, bodily awareness of all these things - where and how you sense them with and within your body. For example, be aware of the inner voice you hear speaking thoughts in your head, of the inner ear with which you hear them, and different sensual textures and qualities of your bodily self-awareness.

3. Concentrate on sensing *where* you feel particular mental states, moods or emotions with and within your body and *how* – which is not *as* mental-emotional states but as purely *sensual* textures and qualities of your bodily self-experience.

4. Remind yourself that the awareness of an object, sensation, emotion or thought is not *itself* an object, sensation, emotion or thought – that it is innately *free* of all objects, sensations, emotions and thoughts. For awareness as such is both inseparable and absolutely distinct from all we are aware of.

5. With this mantra or reminder in mind do not identify with anything in particular that you are aware *of* – but rather with the simple, pure *awareness* of it. Feel how this pure awareness embraces and transcends everything you are aware of – in just the same way that the space around you embraces and yet transcends every thing within it.

6. Sense the very space, light and air around you as a pure space, light and air *of* awareness – one that permeates every atom and cell of your body and pervades the physical space around it. Sense yourself breathing in the pure space, light and air of awareness through every pore of your skin and into a hollow space in your diaphragm – the heart of the divine awareness within you.

7. Sense your whole body and self as nothing but a manifestation of the space around it – of the pure space, light and air of awareness itself. Remind yourself that this is the divine source of your being, your body and of everything and everyone you are aware of within and around you. Thus, experiencing your body and self as an expression of the divine awareness you unite or 'join' with it – the meaning of 'yoga' and the aim of yoga meditation.

The Basic Practice of Awareness (2)

1. Close your eyes, and simply feel the fleshly, physical warmth pervading your body.

2. Now take time to simply be aware of all the muscles you are using to breathe – those of your ribcage, back, diaphragm and abdomen. Through them feel how deep or shallow, rapid or slow your breathing is – and let it be that way. Do not wilfully alter your breathing in any way unless or until a spontaneous bodily impulse to do so arises.

3. Now take time to grant awareness to different areas of your inwardly felt body. In particular any regions of your body where you have any sense of dis-ease or discomfort, whether in the form of a muscular tension, emotional anxiety or discomfort, fatigue or over-fullness, dullness or density.

4. Staying aware of your breathing, and taking time to grant awareness to different regions of your body in turn, allow yourself to feel how in doing so it is as if you are inwardly airing your body with your awareness and your breathing, so that its felt inner space begins to feel purified, clear and translucent.

5. Be aware too of any thoughts, recollections, images or concepts that arise in your mind whilst meditating. Remind yourself that any moods, emotions or sensations you are aware of in your body are in turn an awareness of something to do with your personal life and world as a whole. Meditating your immediate bodily self-awareness, let whatever it calls to mind in relation to your life world as a whole come to mind.

6. Allow yourself to regularly return your awareness to any regions of your body wherever you still feel a sense of dis-ease, until the awareness itself begins to dissipate it, letting the manner of your breathing change in any way you feel helpful.

7. Help this dissipation and clearing process by now becoming more aware of your body as a whole, using your whole body surface to sense the air and space around you, and any scents or sounds in it.

8. Sustaining this awareness of your body and sensing the space and air around it, meditate on feeling your whole body – and every aspect of your self that you experience within it - as a manifestation of that surrounding air and space.

9. Do not identify with any thoughts, images, emotions or bodily sensations but with the pure awareness of them and feel this pure awareness as the very space around them, distinct from and yet embracing and manifesting as everything within it, including your own body.

10. Feel the clear light, space and air of pure awareness pervading the spaces of every atom, molecule and cell of your body as you breathe. In this way begin to feel your breathing as a breathing of the pure air or aether of awareness through every pore of your skin.

11. Be aware in particular of the region of your diaphragm, and feel yourself breathing the pure light, space and air of awareness into a hollow space within it. Sense this space as the very heart of the Divine Awareness within you.

12. Experiment with feeling your body as nothing bounded by your flesh but as boundless space, as light, as air, as fiery flame - and finally again, as simple warmth felt within the safe containing womb of your flesh.

Summary

1. AWARENESS AND EXPERIENCING ARE DISTINCT

There is what is 'going on' right now, all that you are experiencing and whatever it is you are doing, thinking, feeling, saying etc. And there is the awareness of what is going on – the awareness of all you are experiencing and whatever it is you are doing, thinking, feeling, saying etc. This awareness embraces not just what is happening in the here and now but its larger where and larger when – the overall situation and larger life context within which it is going on, goes on, and out of which it is emerging. Ultimately this awareness is a divine-universal awareness embracing and pervading all of space and time.

To 'meditate' is to give ourselves time to identify with the pure AWARENESS of all that we are experiencing – all that is 'going on' – and not with any element or aspect of it.

That is why the truly aware person does not think to themselves 'I think this' or 'I feel that' but rather 'There is an awareness in me of this thought' or 'There is an awareness in me of this feeling'. Thus they would not think 'I feel glad' or 'I feel sad' but rather 'There is an awareness of gladness in me' or 'There is an awareness of sadness in me'.

The first thing a truly aware person does if they feel even the slightest sense of physical, emotional or mental discomfort or 'dis-ease' is to not to seek to distract themselves from it or give it less awareness but, on the contrary to give it more awareness – full awareness – feeling it as pure quality of bodily sensation. Only in this way can they come to identify with the pure awareness of the discomfort or dis-ease rather than identifying – unawares – with that discomfort or dis-ease.

2. AWARENESS IS INNATELY THOUGHT-FREE

We do not need to effortfully 'empty', 'clear', 'free' or 'purify' our minds of thoughts in order to enjoy a meditative space of pure thought-free awareness.

That is because the awareness of a thought is not itself a thought - and thus innately thought-free.

The awareness of a thought or of any 'thing' – whether a sensation or perception, emotion or impulse, need or desire, impulse or action – is not itself a thought or any thing, and therefore innately thought-free and thing-free.

AWARENESS as such, being distinct in principle from each and every element of our experience, each and every 'thing' we are aware of, is innately thought- and thing-free. That is why AWARENESS is FREEDOM.

3. EVERYTHING IS AN AWARENESS

A sensation or perception, need or desire, thought or feeling for example, is not simply something we are aware OF. It is itself an AWARENESS of something or someone else.

Similarly, things in the crude sense are not mere insentient objects. A rock or tree too, is not just something we are aware OF. Instead it IS an awareness in its own right. Cells, molecules atoms and particles of all shapes and forms are expressions of patterns of cellular, molecular and atomic AWARENESS, each with its own particle nature or particularity.

The most self-evident empirical and scientific 'fact' is not the objective EXISTENCE of things but a (subjective) AWARENESS of them. The most basic fact of individual life is not our own existence or being but an intimate and primordial AWARENESS of being.

4. GOD IS AWARENESS

What we call 'God' is not a supreme being 'with' awareness. Instead God IS awareness - an awareness absolute and unbounded, one that is not the private property of any being but the Divine source of all beings. All things and all beings are a part of God - unique, individualised portions of the Divine Universal Awareness that IS God.

5. AWARENESS HAS NO 'CAUSES' OR 'EXPLANATIONS'

To seek the cause of 'consciousness' or 'awareness' in the body or brain is like seeking the 'cause' of a dream and of dreaming as such, in some particular thing we happen to dream of. Awareness cannot – in principle – be explained by or reduced to the property or product of any thing we are aware of, whether awake or dreaming.

6. AWARENESS IS NOT OUR PRIVATE PROPERTY

Awareness is no more private property than space or time. Yet both science and religion are permeated by the unquestioned assumption that awareness is the PRIVATE PROPERTY of individual persons or beings - human or divine – or else the mere PRODUCT of some 'thing' such as the body and brain.

7. AWARENESS IS THE 1ST PRINCIPLE OF ALL THAT IS

'The Awareness Principle' is the recognition that AWARENESS as such ('pure awareness') IS the 1st principle of the universe – the ultimate reality behind and within all things. That is because awareness as such cannot – IN PRINCIPLE – be reduced to or explained by anything we are aware OF. For awareness AS SUCH is the pre-condition or 'field condition' for our consciousness OF anything at all.

8. SPACE AND TIME ARE DIMENSIONS OF AWARENESS

What we are aware of as space is but a spacious field OF AWARENESS - one unrestricted and unbound by anything we are aware of within it.

SPACE IS THE FIELD OF AWARENESS IN WHICH THINGS APPEAR OR BECOME PRESENT TO US AS PHENOMENA.

TIME IS THE MANIFESTATION OR PRESENCING OF PHENOMENA IN THE FIELD OF AWARENESS WE CALL 'SPACE'.

'Time' is the very space of awareness, more or less contracted, pressured and stressed, that we feel within the Moment. 'Space' is the TIME we give ourselves to open up and expand the freedom and spaciousness of the awareness we feel in the Moment.

Only by giving ourselves TIME TO BE AWARE can we expand the TIME-SPACE of our awareness and breathe freely within it – giving ourselves 'breathing space'.

EXPANDING THE SPACIOUSNESS OF OUR AWARENESS ALLOWS US TO BREATHE THE VITALITY OF AWARENESS THAT FILLS SPACE.

9. AWARENESS IS VITAL AIR AND BREATH

SENSING THAT WITH EACH BREATH YOU ARE BREATHING IN THROUGH YOUR ENTIRE BODY SURFACE, YOU ARE ABLE TO ABSORB AND FEEL THIS VITALITY FILLING YOU.

Whether we call it PRANA, CHI, KI or REIKI this subtle 'energy' is nothing but the immanent vitality of pure awareness as such, present throughout space. Only one method of breathing allows us to instantly draw this spiritual vitality into our body – by sensing the infinity of cosmic space around us and feeling as if we are drawing or 'breathing' its vitality in through our entire body surface - that is to say, through every pore of our skin and into every cell of our body.

The skin is our principal organ of respiration. That is why no method of breathing involving only the inner anatomical organs of breath – nose, mouth, diaphragm and lungs can draw on the vitality of pure awareness that surrounds us as space.

10. THE EGOIC 'I' SUBSTITUTES FOR AWARENESS

Through the use of the single word 'I' - indeed in the very act of uttering it in speech, the ego seizes upon, grasps and appropriates all experiencing as its own personal private property - saying to itself and others: "I think this" or "I feel that". The ego's delusion of owning its experience is the essential block to higher awareness known in the yogic tradition as Anavamala. In owning or appropriating all experiencing for itself, the ego both traps our everyday self in identification with 'its' personal experiencing, and expropriates that experiencing from that trans-personal awareness that is its divine source - and the ultimate experiencer.

That is why if, when instead of thinking "'I' think or thought this" or "'I' feel or felt that" we recognise and recall, sense and say to ourselves "THERE IS OR WAS AN AWARENESS OF THINKING THIS" or "THERE IS OR WAS AN AWARENESS OF FEELING THAT", we prevent the egoic 'I' from appropriating experience as its private property.

No writings on attaining higher awareness or enlightenment have yet pointed out the profound connection between the Yogic understanding of 'Anavamala' – the ego's delusion of owning its experience, identity and body as private property - and Marx's understanding of the role of property relations in shaping human consciousness.

'Enlightenment' is not the destruction of the ego as such but transcendence of the PROPRIETORIAL or POSSESIVE ego – that 'I' which takes conscious experiencing as its 'own' activity, takes all experiences as its private property – and treats 'its' body and brain as a material 'means of production' of experience.

In Marxist terms, overcoming Anavamala means allowing awareness to 'expropriate the expropriator' – the capitalist or 'bourgeois' ego. When this happens the ego itself ceases to take itself as the experiencing self and owner of its experiences. Instead it becomes just one aspect of an experienced self among others – a self that that there is an awareness of experiencing.

Out of this trans-personal awareness of experiencing comes an entirely new experience of awareness and an entirely new experience of self - an experience of that Self that is awareness and of that awareness which is our deepest Self - identical with the Divine. The liberated ego no longer immediately seizes upon, grasps, owns and 'appropriates' its experiencing as 'our' own. Instead it is itself 'enowned' - reowned and reappropriated by that trans-personal awareness which is our divine Self.

THE LIBERATED EGO OR 'I' KNOWS ITSELF SOLELY AS A MINDER OR 'CARETAKER' OF THAT AWARENESS OUT OF WHICH ALL EXPERIENCING ARISES - NOT ITS OWNER.

The higher truth is that it is not 'we' that experience or 'have' experiences, nor 'we' that experience or 'have' a self. Instead all experiencing, including our self-experience, belongs to and arises from the Divine Awareness - as

ITS self-expression and ITS self-experience. To be able, in everyday speech and communication, to utter the word 'I' in this sense - from out of an awareness transcending it is the highest and most demanding accomplishment in the Practice of Awareness that is The New Yoga of Awareness.

11. FREEDOM IS AWARE ACTION

Free action is aware action because only out of awareness comes mindfulness of more than one possible action and free choice between them.

Every single thing you do without first giving time to be aware of what else you might best do at this time, how else or in what other manner you might best do it, and when else might be the best time to do it – every such act is an unaware and unfree act.

Unaware action is unfree action because it does not come out of an awareness of alternative 'whats', 'hows' and 'whens' - and therefore is not an act of free choice but rather one determined solely by ego or impulse.

12. AWARE ACTION IS RIGHT ACTION

Aware action is right action because it comes from giving ourselves time to weigh up and feel out the rightness of different possible actions in awareness – and let awareness decide rather than ego or impulse. Action positively 'decided' by the ego without meditative awareness is itself mere reaction to external events and surrender to inner impulses.

Whether we act impulsively, 'in the heat of the moment', or use reason to coolly rationalise our actions, makes no difference. For if we do act and speak without meditative awareness and mindfulness of alternative possible deeds and words, all our actions remain unaware, unfree and purely reactive. Unaware, un-pre-meditated actions are like actions engaged in 'spontaneously' in a dream – without the lucidity and freedom of choice that comes from awareness that we are dreaming.

MORE ON THE PRACTICE OF AWARENESS

The Traditional Practice

Verily, what is called Brahman – that is the same as what the space outside a person is. Verily, what the space outside a person is, that is the same as what the space within a person is – that is the same as what the space here within the heart is. That is the fullness, the quiescent.

The Chandogya Upanishad

As the mighty air which pervades everything, ever abides
in space, know that in the same way all beings abide in Me.

The Bhagavad Gita

Meditate on space as omnipresent and free of all limitations.
Think 'I am not my own body. I exist everywhere'.
Meditate on one's own body as the universe and as having the nature of awareness.
Meditate on the skin as being like an outer wall with nothing within it.
Meditate on the void in one's body extending in all directions simultaneously.
Meditate on one's own self as a vast unlimited expanse.
Meditate on a bottomless well or as standing in a very high place.
Meditate on the void above and the void below.
Meditate on the bodily elements as pervaded with voidness.
Contemplate that the same awareness exists in all bodies.
Whether outside or inside Shiva [pure awareness] is omnipresent.

The yogi should contemplate the entirety of open space (or sky) as the essence of Bhairava [Shiva]...
One should, setting aside identification with one's own body, contemplate that the same awareness is present in other bodies than one's own.

The Vijnanabhairavatantra

...the power of space [Akasha-Shakti] is inherent in the soul as true subjectivity, which is at once empty of objects and which also provides a place in which objects may be known.

Abhinavagupta's Tantraloka

Meditation as a Practice of Awareness

Many people think, for one reason or another, that they should 'do' something that they call 'meditation'. What they have in mind is maybe going to a meditation class of some sort or 'doing' some form of purely physical 'yoga'. Whether or not they do so however, 'meditation', understood in this way, is taken as just another thing to 'do' – and therefore also just another thing to make time for in their busy or stressful lives. This is a paradox, for the true meaning of meditation does not lie in adding to the list of things we need to make time to do. Indeed, the true meaning of meditation does not lie in making time to 'do' anything at all, nor even making time just to 'be' in some ambiguous way. Instead the meaning of meditation lies in making time *to be aware*. Not at some future time but here and now, and in every moment of our lives.

There is what is 'going on' right now … whatever it is you are doing, thinking, feeling, saying etc. And there is *the awareness* of what is going on – the awareness of whatever it is you are doing, thinking, feeling, saying etc. This awareness embraces not just what is happening in the here and now but its larger *where* and larger *when* – the overall situation and larger life context *within* which it is going on, goes on, and out of which it is emerging. Ultimately it is an awareness that embraces all of space and time.

We say that some people are more sensitive or 'aware' than others. What we mean is that they are generally aware of *more* than others are – more aspects of what is going on, whether in themselves or in others, in the world at large or in the here and now. Those with lesser awareness may have a need to *express* themselves more – for example through therapy - merely to discover just how much more there is for them to be aware of. Those with greater awareness however, may have a no lesser need to express themselves – needing to share all that they may be aware of with others in order not to feel overwhelmed or isolated by that awareness. Both communication and creativity themselves are seen as ways of *giving out* through self-expression, rather than as occasions for fully taking others in, whether through the word or in receptive silence.

As a result, people's social interaction consists simply of talk and telling stories - everyone sharing in words, each for themselves, what is most important to them, whilst their private life is either mute, uncreative and expressionless or else an ongoing search for some form of highly personal self-expression. The fact is however, that we do not need to share all of which we are aware, for awareness itself communicates and transmits itself silently, wordlessly, needing no form of outward expression.

Whether their awareness is greater or lesser, most people have a tendency to identify it with whatever it is they are aware *of*. Not understanding the true nature of awareness they take it as their *own* – as the private property of their ego or 'I'. This is reflected in common ways of speaking. If for example, we are aware of a thought or feeling what we think to ourselves or say to others is '*I* think this' or '*I* feel that'. In doing so we identify ('I-dentify') with whatever it is we are aware *of*. Meditation demands that we overcome the misconception that awareness as such – what is called pure awareness – is something that is 'ours', that is 'yours' or 'mine' – and thus the personal property of our ego or 'I'.

To enter a true state of *meditative* awareness however – to 'meditate' - is the opposite of 'I-dentifying' with any thing or things we are aware of.

To meditate is to give ourselves time to identify with the pure awareness of what is going on – and not with any element or aspect of it.

That is why the truly aware person on the other hand, does not think '*I* think this' or '*I* feel that', '*I* recall this' or '*I* would like that'. Instead, were it put into words, their *experience* of awareness would not begin with the word 'I' but with the words 'There is..'. They would not think to themselves '*I* think this' or 'I feel that' but rather '*There is an awareness* in me of this thought' or '*There is an awareness* in me of this feeling'. Thus they would not think 'I feel tired' or 'I feel anxious' but rather '*There is an awareness* of tiredness in me' or '*There is an awareness* of anxiety in me'. This is important, because the foundation of all meditation is the understanding that the awareness of a thought or feeling, mood or emotion, impulse or activity, need or desire, *is not itself* a thought or feeling, mood or emotion, impulse or activity, need or desire, but is instead something innately free of all these elements of our experiencing. For just as our awareness of a thing such as a table is not itself a thing, not itself a table, so is our awareness of a thought not itself a thought. Instead it is something innately thought free. Thus we do not need to effortfully 'empty', 'clear' or 'free' our mind of thoughts in order to reach a state of pure thought-free awareness. On the contrary, all we need do is identify with the pure awareness of our thoughts. The same applies to all elements of our experience, all so-called contents of consciousness. We do not need to empty our consciousness of these contents in order to achieve a state of awareness free of attachment to them. For the simple awareness of those contents is itself an awareness free from and unattached to them.

Meditation then, is based on the recognition that awareness as such – pure awareness – is not bound or restricted to any particular thing or things we are aware *of* – whether in the form of thoughts or feelings, impulses or sensations, needs or desires, memories or anticipations. Instead, it is like *space* – for though space is inseparable from the objects in it, it also remains absolutely distinct from them, and is not itself any 'thing'. Pure awareness, quite simply, is a clear and empty space *of* awareness – for whilst it embraces everything we experience, it remains absolutely distinct from each and every element of our experience, each and every 'thing' we are aware *of*.

To not get lost, stressed, drained, depressed or fatigued by whatever is going on - whatever we might be doing or saying, thinking or feeling – demands only that we stop identifying with the immediate *focus* of our awareness and identify instead with the larger space or *field* of awareness around it. What we ordinarily call 'consciousness' is a type of highly focused or focal awareness. True *awareness* on the other hand is a type of non-focal, non-local or *field consciousness*. As long as people are identified with the immediate focus of their awareness whether external or internal, they remain as if *encapsulated* in a bubble from which no amount of social interaction and communication will free them – for all this allows them is the relief of *self-expression* of whatever it is they are aware of from within their respective bubbles. Paradoxically, freedom from such encapsulation in ourselves and in what we think of as 'our' awareness can be attained only by granting more awareness to our most *fleshly* capsule – our skin – using it to sense the larger space *around* our heads and bodies. For that larger space is in essence but a larger field or space *of awareness*. It is by identifying with this larger space that we identify with the *pure awareness* of all that is going on - whether within or between our own 'bubbles' of awareness and those of others.

Expanding our *awareness of space* then, is the key to *experiencing* awareness itself *as* an expansive, all-embracing and transcendent space – embracing and transcending not just our own body but that of every thing and person within it. By sensing and identifying with an expanded awareness of space, we cease to experience awareness as something encapsulated in our minds or brains or bounded by our own skin.

To truly be *aware* is to literally be *in* awareness – to experience ourselves abiding or dwelling within a spacious field of pure awareness in the same way as our bodies abide and dwell within space. That spacious expanse of the pure awareness in which we all dwell is not 'ours', not 'yours' nor 'mine', and yet it is the very essence of the divine. For as it is written in the Bhagavad Gita:

As the mighty Air that pervades everything ever abides in Space, know that in the same way all Beings abide in Me.

We all seek 'breathing space' in our busy lives. To 'meditate' is to identify with *the pure awareness* of all that is going on. This means sensing and identifying with the larger field or *space* within which it goes on. In this way we begin to feel more *breathing* space – not by breathing fresh air or by doing exercises in 'breath control' but by literally breathing in the very 'air-ness' of pure awareness itself - that 'higher air' or 'aether' which pervades all things, yet abides in the seeming emptiness of the space around them.

To begin with however, all we need 'do' to meditate is to give ourselves time to grant full awareness to our *bodies* - allowing ourselves to be as fully aware as possible of any elements of anxiety, stress, tension, restlessness or dis-ease, however subtle or intense, that we sense within them. By giving awareness to our bodies in this way, we can, at the same time, give time to become more aware of things going on in our lives that may be 'on our mind' or that 'come to mind' as conscious mental thoughts or concerns directly related to what we are feeling in our bodies. The longer we do this, the more time we give ourselves *to be aware* – first of all of our bodies as a whole and then of all that preoccupies our minds – the more we will sense a gap opening up between our body-mind and the everyday self it constitutes and the very awareness we are granting it. In this way we begin to feel a gap between our everyday self and identity and another deep self – that Self which is *granting awareness* to our everyday self and lives, that Self, which, in its essence *is* the awareness we are granting.

When we begin to sense that second, deeper Self we take the second major step in meditation. If the first step is giving ourselves time to be aware, the second is passing from 'being aware' to 'being awareness'. This means ceasing to identify with anything we are aware *of* in our bodies and minds, but identifying instead with that very *awareness* we are giving ourselves, and with the Self that *is* that awareness, our 'awareness self' (the 'Atman').

Feeling that Self 'immanently' – from deep down inside or within our bodies – we can then begin to feel it 'transcendentally'. This is the third stage of meditation. We reach it by giving awareness not just to all that is going on inside us – in the inner spaces of our bodies and within our minds – but also to our skin surface, using it to sense more intensely the clear empty space surrounding our heads and bodies. As we expand our awareness into that space we begin to feel it as an infinite space *of* awareness – of which not just our body but all bodies are but different shapes or expressions. All that we were previously more intensely aware of as 'going' on in our body and mind – indeed in our everyday life in its entirety – we now experience as nothing more than shallow ripples and reflections on the surface of a fathomless, underground ocean of awareness. At the same time, we feel the deeper Self within us as one centre of a vast, vaulting *time-space* of awareness – one that spans our entire lifetime.

It is *as and from* this Self that we can give ourselves time to 'meditate' at any time, simply by giving more awareness to all that is going on within us or pre-occupying our bodies and minds – whilst at the same time 'breathing' the pure air or 'aether' of that clear, contentless awareness which surrounds us as space itself, and that spans all of time.

Meditation, Movement and 'Just Sitting'

'Meditation', as understood through The Awareness Principle, means simply giving *time-space* to a type of wholly non-active or 'quiescent' awareness – one not reliant on bodily movement or action. Most Westerners however, can only feel a sense of meditative inner stillness through movement in space.

Sitting still, they can no longer feel their body as a whole, let alone sense the space of awareness, around it – but instead begin to get lost in thought and their heads. Put in other terms, they cannot sustain a 'proprioceptive' awareness of their own body without sensations of physical movement – without 'kinaesthetic' awareness.

That is why they need to be constantly 'on the move' – whether through any type of physical activity involving movement of the body, or by literally moving from place to place - for example by travelling or engaging in pursuits such as walking, jogging, swimming etc.

That is also why a notable guru of the nineteen sixties and seventies felt forced to come up with the idea of so-called 'dynamic meditation' – effectively no form of meditation at all but a mere means of emotional catharsis through spontaneous movement.

Kinaesthetic awareness – dependent on movement – does indeed awaken proprioceptive awareness. Yet in Western culture it is, for most people, the *only* way they know of awakening or sustaining proprioceptive awareness of their bodies.

In Eastern and aboriginal cultures the reverse has been traditionally the case – movement and *kinaesthetic* awareness are grounded in motionless stillness and *proprioceptive* awareness of one's body.

As in the practice of Tai Chi and of different forms of Asian dance and martial art, Eastern cultures value forms of bodily movement which arise out of a sense of motionless stillness – and believe in letting this very motionless stillness guide and time their physical movement or 'kinesis'. Thus the most truly advanced martial artist is precisely one who does not actively move their body at all, but rather lets it *be moved* – moved by a 'proprioceptive' awareness that embraces not only their body but their sense of the entire space around their body.

It is because the 'kinaesthetic' awareness of the martial artist is *already* so highly trained that all they require to guide their physical movements is a meditative, motionless proprioceptive awareness.

Sitting meditation on the other hand, teaches people how to 'move' in a different way – to move from one location or 'place' to another *in themselves* - not with their physical body but *within* their inwardly felt body.

Strictly speaking this is not movement at all but *awareness* – awareness of the many different sensations and feelings and thoughts that are presencing or *occurring* in different regions or locations of their body. It is awareness too, of the relation of these sensations or feelings, whether subtle or intense, to the thoughts they are having and to the things or people they are connected with in their world.

The principle aim of sitting meditation is to learn how to be physically still whilst still sustaining awareness of our body as a whole and the space around it - sustaining both proprioceptive and spatial awareness.

This proprioceptive awareness is what sitting meditation and the Zen practice of 'just sitting' was implicitly designed to cultivate. Yet the problems faced by students of Zen-style sitting meditation – physical restlessness, mental boredom or drifting off, were not understood and responded to with this understanding or aim in mind – the aim of cultivating awareness of our bodies and the space around them.

Instead they were left to struggle with sensations of restlessness, strain, boredom or fatigue leading them to mentally dissociate from their bodies rather than become more aware of them, to get lost in thought or even fall asleep during meditation – hence the Master's 'awakening' stick. There was no instruction to students to fully *affirm* all bodily sensations in awareness – thus coming to recognise that the very *awareness* of a bodily sensation is not itself anything bodily but is essentially *bodiless* and *sensation-free*.

Similarly the *awareness* of a distracting thought or mental state is not itself anything mental or any activity of mind – 'mindfulness' – but is instead something essentially *thought- and mind-free*.

Lacking this understanding and experience of pure awareness, Zen students were left to rely on their minds to distract or dissociate themselves from their bodies - or to simply stay awake. This however only compounded the challenge of attaining a state of pure, mind- and thought-free awareness.

What they required was 'The Awareness Principle' – the recognition that just as the awareness of our bodies and of bodily sensations is not itself anything bodily, so is the pure awareness of our minds and thoughts not itself anything mental but a thought and mind-free awareness.

The Zen *practice* of sitting meditation aimed at transcending both mind and body and attaining a state called emptiness or *mu* – 'No mind. No body.' Yet this practice did not recognise that the pure *awareness* of mind and body is – *in principle* - something innately transcendent or free of body and mind.

Without this recognition, 'success' in meditation came to be identified more and more with 'one-pointedness' – the *concentration* of awareness on a single inner or outer focal point (for example the centre of a *mandala.*). It is precisely this practice of 'one-pointedness' however, that *misses the point* – which is that a state of pure mind- and body-free awareness is, in contrast to ordinary consciousness, precisely an awareness *not* focussed or concentrated on a single, localised point. Instead it is an all-round 'field' awareness embracing the entirety of space – not least the space around our bodies, around our physical sensations and around our thoughts themselves.

It is from the *formless all-round space of pure awareness* that all formed elements of our bodily and mental experiencing, inner and outer, arise. To concentrate 'single-pointedly' on any one of these is to miss the central aim of meditation, which is to cultivate a proprioceptive *awareness* of our bodies – and even our thoughts themselves - from the space surrounding them.

The term 'sacred space' is both true and misleading. For a sacred space or a holy place such as a temple or cathedral, is in essence any place which helps us – either through its vast inner or outer dimensions and/or through its association with God or the divine – to experience space as such *as* sacred and holy – *as* the divine and *as* the God inside which we dwell.

What happens when people enter a sacred space such as a large cathedral for example is - first of all - that they gain a sense of its vaulting spaciousness, and at the same time, by virtue of knowing the cathedral as a holy place or 'house of God' - associate this spaciousness with that holiness and with God.

When people come together in temples, churches or mosques they are first of all aware of being together in a common space which is recognised as sacred or holy in some way. In that way, they knowingly or unknowingly come to an experience of space itself as divine – that which embraces all things and beings. *Going* to a holy place involves movement in space. Yet *being there* means motionlessly abiding in that place, thus coming to experiencing its space – and thereby space itself – as holy.

Again, movement or *kinesis* – activity or change of place – can be a way of awakening or sustaining proprioceptive awareness, or it can be a way of avoiding it. Yet the question whether, at any given moment, awareness is better sustained through movement or non-movement, can itself only be decided by first of all *not*-moving – by abiding in a motionless stillness.

Mountains and trees do not move from place to place, go to church, go for walks or go on pilgrimages. Mountains will not come to Mohammed. Trees do not have eyes to see. Yet they are the true '*Zen* masters' and *yogis* of nature. For not having eyes to perceive space or limbs by which to move from place to place, they are masters at motionlessly sensing the space, light and air around them. Indeed their proprioceptive sense of their own bodies comes from sensing their spatiality.

The tree's trunk rises towards the heights of the sky. Its roots plumb the depths of the earth. Its branches spread and its leaves and flowers open themselves to the vaulting curvature of the heavens above – absorbing the light and air of space not through any eyes or noses, but through their *entire surface*.

To be 'conscious' is to be aware of things occurring – abiding or moving - 'in' the space around them. To be *aware* of things however, is not the same as to *be* that very awareness. To *be* awareness means to *be* the space, inner and outer, in which things occur, and not just be aware of things occurring in that space. For pure awareness, in our space-time reality, *is* space. Being *space*, we do not need to engage in activity or movement to experience *time*. For space is *time-space*. The vaulting expanse of space *is* the spacious expanse of time itself – a time-space that embraces all actions and places - past, present and future - without any need for movement from one place to another 'in' space or one moment to another 'in' time.

Practicing Sitting as Meditation

Sitting meditation is essentially the experience of sitting – anywhere and anytime - *as* meditation. This involves 4 simple steps:

1. Sitting with your eyes open, but not looking at anything.

2. Sustaining awareness of your sensed body surface as a whole.

3. Feeling your body surface as 'all eye' – enabling you to sense the entire space within and all around your body.

4. Letting all that you are aware of within your body in the form of sensations or feelings and all that comes to mind in the form of thoughts and images dissipate into the space around your body.

Practicing Spatial Awareness

The most fundamental Practice of Awareness is the practice of sustaining continuous 'whole-body awareness' throughout the day. The foundation of this whole-body awareness is awareness of one's felt body surface as a whole. For without awareness of our surface we can feel neither the inner *space of awareness* it bounds and surrounds nor the awareness that *is the outer* space surrounding it – these being the two distinct but inseparable aspects of the 'awareness space' that make up our 'awareness body' or 'soul body'. Surface awareness is thus the key to experiencing 'whole-body' awareness as 'soul-body' awareness. Sustaining this whole-body/soul-body awareness through spatial body awareness can only be achieved through constant mindfulness and regular recall of the following twelve questions – all of which have to do and affect how much space one feels one has – both for oneself and for others.

Meditating Awareness as Space

1. How much of my body surface am I feeling right now?

2. How much inner awareness space can I feel within this felt surface boundary?

3. Where do I feel my awareness concentrated in this inner awareness space?

4. Where do I feel my awareness centred in this inner-bodily awareness space?

5. How far down does my inner awareness space extend from the inner space of my head through that of my chest to my lower abdomen?

6. How expansive or contracted, crowded or empty, muddied or clear, do I feel the inner awareness space of my head, chest and abdomen?

7. To what extent do I feel the inner awareness space of head, chest and abdomen as a singular inner space of awareness?

8. To what extent can I lower my centre of awareness from a point in my head to points in the inner region of my heart, diaphragm, belly and lower abdomen?

9. To what extent can I sense the entire space around my body surface?

10. How far can I feel my awareness extending into this space?

11. To what extent can I feel the entire space around me as an unbounded space of awareness enveloping and embracing both my own body and every other body in it?

12. How permeable or impermeable do I feel the surface boundary between my inner and outer awareness spaces - to what extent can I feel my surface boundary as either a porous in-breathing membrane or as a sealed self-containing boundary?

'Akasha Yoga' and 'Khechari Mudra'

Among the various meanings of 'Mudra' are 'to seal' and 'to rejoice' or 'give joy'. In the old-new Practice of Awareness which I call 'The New Yoga of Awareness', a Mudra is not simply a gesture of the hand but any bodily gesture or comportment, which serves to fix or 'seal' a particular meditative inner stance or 'bearing'. It is a way of relating to or 'comporting' oneself in relation to both outer and inner space – whether through one's bodily posture or stance as a whole, through a look on one's face or in one's eyes, or through a gesture of one's arms, hands and fingers. That is why what was called 'Khechari Mudra' is referred to in the *tantras* as one of *the* most important meditative inner stances or bearings – allowing as it does a rejoicing (Sanskrit 'mud') in the experience of space (KHA) as a field of pure awareness flowing with currents of its own air-like or 'aetheric' substantiality (AKASHA). 'Khechari' means 'moving in the void' or 'she [the goddess] who moves in the void' – this void being no vacuum but the infinite field of pure awareness or cosmic aether that we ordinarily perceive *only* as 'empty' physical or cosmic space.

As an expansion of awareness in space, Khechari Mudra expresses the root meaning of 'tan-tra' – to guard or protect ('trai') awareness by spreading, extending or expanding it ('tan'). The term 'Khechari' itself derives from the Indo-European root KHE or KHA, from which arises also the Greek term KHAOS – misunderstood as 'chaos'. The starting point of Khechari Mudra is identification with space itself, both the space around and surrounding our bodies and the sensed inner spaces of our bodies – rather than with anything at all that we are aware of or experience within those spaces. This leads to a new experience of space as something identical with pure awareness itself.

Only through The Practice of Awareness that is Khechari Mudra can we *experience* the distinction, fundamental to The Awareness Principle, between awareness as such and anything we are aware of – whether thoughts, feelings, physical sensations, our own bodies, or the bodies of objects and people around us. This in turn frees us from being or becoming identified in an unaware way with any elements of our outer or inner life-world or experience. As a practice of identifying with, breathing and moving in the apparent emptiness of space, Khechari Mudra is both a 'Yoga of Space' ('Akasha Yoga') and a Yoga of the Breath ('Prana Yoga'). It leads us to a state of total equanimity in which, like the vaulting sky itself (Vyoman) we can rise above all mundane, earthly experiencing – feeling ourselves as the very space that surrounds all bodies, and feeling how, as space, we also pervade them like a subtle 'aetheric' air, wind or breath (Prana).

Expanding Spatial Awareness - 'Khechari Mudra'

Note: this meditation is to be practiced in the true *tantric* manner – attending to your 'inner space' but with your eyes still open. This is so that you can stay aware of the entire space around you ('Bhairava Mudra'), expanding your awareness into that space and experiencing everything in it as an expression of it. This practice of Khechari Mudra – uniting the Kingdom outside with the Kingdom inside – is the key to all the miraculous 'Siddhis' exercised by great Yogis, Gurus and Avatars.

1. Bring your awareness to the inwardly sensed surface of your chest and body as a whole. From that surface sense the empty spaces in front of, above, behind and to either side of your body.

2. Attend entirely to your awareness of regions of empty space - those above and around your body, and those above, around and between other bodily objects or people.

3. Be aware of the sky above and of the unlimited expanse of cosmic space, and of all empty regions of space in your immediate vicinity or scope of vision.

4. Sense all regions of 'empty' space as part of an unlimited space of pure awareness – a space totally untainted by any psychical qualities, be they the 'atmosphere' of places, the 'aura' of people and the mood or 'space' you or others may feel themselves in.

5. Feel your body surface again, this time sensing a hollow space of pure awareness within it – a space equally untainted by any thoughts, feelings or sensations you experience within it.

6. Identify with the spaces of awareness around and between all that you experience outside and inside you – the space around and between your thoughts, emotions and physical sensations, the space around and between your body and other bodies.

7. Attend to your breathing, and feel yourself breathing in the luminous translucency of the space around you, first through your chest and body surface as a whole - experiencing this as a breathing of pure awareness.

8. Feel your chest and body surface as an open, porous, in-breathing skin or membrane uniting a content-free space of pure awareness within you with the 'empty' space of pure awareness surrounding your own body and all other bodies.

Aspects of the Practice of Awareness

1. BEING AWARE

Taking all the time necessary to be aware of all you are experiencing inwardly and outwardly, and of every distinct element of your experiencing, from thoughts and feelings, to somatic sensations and every element of your sensory environment.

2. BODILY AWARENESS

Attending to the immediate bodily dimension of all that you are aware of experiencing – where and how you feel different things you perceive or are aware of in an immediate sensual, proprioceptive and bodily way.

3. BODYING AWARENESS

Giving some form of authentic bodily expression to your awareness, for example through your posture, the tilt of your body or head, the look on your face or in your eyes, the tone or tempo of your voice – thus amplifying, bodying and silently communicating your awareness of it.

4. UNBOUNDING YOUR AWARENESS

Reminding yourself that your bodily awareness of your body is not itself bounded by your body, but is an unbounded bodiless awareness that permeates your body, all of space and every body in it.

5. BEING-IN-AWARENESS

You dwell IN awareness as you dwell in space itself. Being-in-Awareness is a way of Being Awareness, by not identifying with what you are aware of, but identifying instead with the very spaces of awareness, inner and outer, *in* which you experience them.

6. BREATHING AWARENESS

Expanding the 'breathing space' of your awareness by giving yourself time to be aware of the way you are - or are not – breathing, by shifting your awareness TO your breathing, and experiencing it as a breathing OF awareness – feeling yourself breathing your awareness of the entire sensory space around you through your chest surface, felt as open and porous.

7. BEING AWARENESS

Being-in, Bodying and Breathing awareness are paths that lead from Being Aware to Being Awareness. Being Awareness means affirming and feeling the meaningfulness of all that you are aware of, whilst not identifying with it but instead identifying with the very awareness of it – BEING that awareness instead of BINDING your awareness to what you are aware of. To BE awareness is to be the all-round SPACE, inner and outer, in which you experience things - including your own body. To identify with AWARENESS as such is to identify with SPACE as such.

8. UNBINDING AWARENESS

Each time you become aware of experiencing something new, step back once again into Being Awareness in order to UNBIND your awareness from it – thus continuing both to Be Aware and to Be Awareness rather than letting your awareness become BOUND by anything you are aware of.

9. BEING-IN-AWARENESS WITH OTHERS

Relating in a meditative way by using every encounter as an opportunity to give yourself time to Be Aware of others, to Breathe in your awareness of them, and to feel the space around you both as a space of awareness in which you can both 'Be in Awareness' together.

10. ATTAINING AWARENESS BLISS

The bliss that arises from recognising that you are not a being with awareness but that you ARE awareness – part of the unbounded awareness that IS 'God'. Awareness Bliss is only attained through Being Aware, Being and Bodying Awareness, Breathing Awareness, and Being in Awareness with others, - breathing the divine awareness that both you and others are.

10 Steps - from Being Aware to Being Awareness

1. Be aware whenever you find yourself thinking or saying to yourself or others 'I *am*...'. For example, 'I *am*... lonely/depressed/anxious/afraid/angry/bitter/worthless/trapped/frustrated/resentful/ashamed/unworthy/ugly/unloved/guilty/bad/mad, a failure etc.

2. Fill in the blank from the words 'I am ...' with your own choice of negative words.

3. Now replace the word 'am' with the words 'feel' and 'think' and say to yourself 'I *feel* ... and *think* I am ...' [fill in your own words]. Do not follow the words 'I feel...' with an emotional label but with a description of your direct *bodily* sensation of the feeling. Example: "I feel a fluttering in my chest which makes me think I am 'anxious'."

4. In order not to identify with your feelings and thoughts now remove the word 'I'. Rather than saying to yourself 'I feel ...', 'I think ...' or 'I am...' say '*There is an awareness* of feeling... which makes me *think* I am...' [fill in your own words]. Again, do not label the feeling as an emotion but describe how you feel it as a bodily sensation.

5. Be aware of your body as a whole and of your *overall mood and sense of yourself* – for it is out of this overall bodily sense of yourself that your thoughts and feelings arise.

6. Feelings and thoughts *about* reality *are not* reality. Feelings and thoughts about yourself *are not* your whole self or true self. So whenever you are aware

of saying 'I am …' remind yourself that 'I am *not* this feeling of…' or 'I am not this thought that …'.

7. Instead say: 'I am the *awareness* of feeling … or thinking …' or 'There is an awareness of feeling … or thinking … '. Make it a rule to use the following mantras: '*There is an awareness* of thinking or feeling …' or '*I am the awareness* of feeling or thinking …'

8. Identifying with a thing or thought, feeling or belief – *unawares* - is one thing. Being *aware* of that thing or thought, feeling or belief – and of the self that is identified with it is another. The point is to *be* that very *awareness* and not anything you are aware of.

9. Whenever you feel preoccupied with disturbing thoughts or feelings, identify with empty space. For empty space, like pure awareness, is distinct from everything we are aware of within it - whether things or thoughts, sensations or feelings, impulses or actions.

10. Regularly take *time* to be fully aware of and affirm all the sensations, feelings, thoughts or life-concerns you are aware *of.* But do not identify with them. Instead, attend to and sense the spaces within and around you and say the following mantras to yourself 'I am nothing that I am aware of in space. I am space itself.' I am nothing I am aware of. I am the pure awareness of it.' Only by regularly *taking time to be aware* can we open up a larger *space of awareness* – one in which new thoughts and feelings, a new sense of yourself and a new relation to the world and other people can and will arise spontaneously. This is the basic life discipline, practice or *yoga* of awareness.

AWARENESS AND HEALING

Awareness and Illness

Subjectively, illness of any sort does not begin with some external or internal cause – some object such as a virus or cancerous cell. Nor does it even necessarily begin with some well-defined experiential symptom such as a localised pain. Instead it begins with an ill-defined *awareness* of 'not feeling ourselves'. It is this awareness of 'not feeling ourselves' that is accompanied by worries and experienced as a sense of 'dis-ease'. And whilst it is common knowledge that illness can 'change' people, what medicine ignores is that the very essence of illness has to do with *identity* – every symptom being subjectively experienced both as an altered *state of consciousness* and as an altered *sense of self*. If ignored, the ill-defined awareness of 'not feeling ourselves' can grow and take the form of a more localised well-defined symptom. 'Scientific' medicine then seeks objective causes and cures for such symptoms. Yet it implicitly retains a subjective element. This is not just because it relies partly on patients' subjective accounts of their symptoms but also because 'cure' – indeed 'health' as such – is understood not just as an absence, or successful elimination or amelioration of symptoms but also as a restored sense of *identity* – 'feeling ourselves' again.

The entire medical understanding of illness and the entire relationship of patient and physician rests on an unspoken agreement to seek something *other than self* (whether an organic cause, traumatic event, or a diagnostically labelled 'disorder') to explain the patient's sense of dis-ease, their awareness of *not feeling themselves*. The basic principle of medicine – 'The Medical Principle' – is based not on *fact* but on (a) the dogmatic *belief* that illness has no intrinsic meaning for the individual and (b) the military *metaphor* of 'fighting' its causes rather than seeking its meaning. In contrast The Awareness Principle offers an approach to illness which begins where it actually begins – the sense of 'dis-ease' which accompanies the awareness of 'not feeling ourselves'. Yet instead of denying meaning to this inwardly felt dis-ease – merely labelling it as a medical disease or disorder and seeking causes for it in something *other than self* - The Practice of Awareness encourages the patient to fully affirm the awareness of *not feeling themselves* as soon as it emerges, and to both *understand* and *transform* it into a quite different awareness – the awareness of *feeling another self*. This can both prevent the ill-defined dis-ease of not feeling oneself from developing into well-defined disease symptoms, or alternatively allow those very symptoms to be experienced in a different way – not simply as an altered mental or physical state but as an altered state of consciousness and with it an altered bodily *sense of self*.

By fully affirming this altered sense of self, we let the essential dis-ease of *not feeling ourselves* achieve its true and most meaningful purpose - that of allowing us to *feel another self* - one we hitherto feared to be aware of or to recognise as part of our *self as a whole* - our 'soul'. And by letting another self express itself in our thoughts and emotions and finding ways to *body* it in our overall demeanour or 'body language', we remove the need to *repress* or medicalise our bodily sense of that self. For then that self will no longer feel forced to *express* itself through bodily symptoms or through behaviours regarded as forms of 'mental' disorder.

We do not 'have' a body. We body 'our-selves'. Our bodies are but the embodiment of the particular way in which we are bodying ourselves – and the particular selves we are bodying. Being aware of an emotion or any aspect of our self-experience and *bodying* it in our demeanour is not the same as 'somatising' it through physical symptoms or giving it free reign to emotionally determine our *behaviour*. Someone who cannot allow themselves to *frown* with anger, adopt an aggressive bearing or give an angry or aggressive *look* to someone – thus silently *embodying* that anger through their demeanour – is more likely to *enact* their anger in their behaviour, expressing it in harsh or hurtful words or deeds. Thus someone who cannot allow themselves to be fully *aware* of their anger and feel it in their bodies - to *be* angry – is more likely to 'get' angry. It is only because we are not taught, like good actors, to first of all *inwardly* feel the selves that find expression in the different 'parts' they act out – without in anyway *judging* them – that we ourselves may feel forced to act those parts in real life, or feel a strong *fear* of doing so. The reason that the actor Anthony Hopkins could so effectively play the gruesome figure of Hannibal Lecter – without becoming or acting like him in real life – is *not* because he distanced himself as a person from the part he played but because he deliberately sought, found and felt the self within him that could fully identify with Hannibal.

People fear to fully feel any 'other selves' that they judge as 'bad' or 'dangerous' in some way – for example mad, violent, sadistic, weak or suicidal selves. The fear is that if they allowed themselves to be more aware of these selves and feel them more fully, they would *become* mad, violent, sadistic, weak, suicidal etc. In reality it is those who fear to feel such selves within themselves who are more likely to end up impulsively 'acting out' these selves in their behaviour. Thus a self that feels violent only actually acts in a violent way through the body if its violence is not fully felt in a bodily way. Actual bodily violence results from a *fear* of violent feelings, and is essentially a last-ditch attempt to *evacuate* violent feelings *from* one's body rather than fully feeling them with and within one's body. Bodily *enactment* of feared emotions, impulses, states and selves replaces a fuller awareness of those emotions, impulses, states and selves. That is a great paradox, for were we to allow ourselves greater awareness, that very awareness would *free* us from those aspects of our bodily self-experience that we fear.

For paradoxically, *awareness* of our bodies is not itself anything bodily but is a bodiless or body-free awareness. Similarly the awareness of our minds is not itself anything 'mental' but is a mind-free awareness. The same basic precept of The Awareness Principle applies to all aspects of our self-experience

– including our thoughts, feelings, fears, sensations, impulses, illnesses and sickness symptoms. Just as *the awareness* of a thought is not itself a thought, and is something essentially thought-free, so also is the awareness of an emotion, sensation, urge or impulse something essentially free of emotions, sensations, urges or impulses. There is nothing sick or ill about the *awareness* of a symptom or the awareness of feeling ill. Similarly, the awareness of a fear is not itself something fearful but is essentially a 'neutral' or fear-free awareness. And just as the awareness of our bodies is nothing bodily, so is the awareness of a particular self not something that binds us to that self – or to any self.

It is only because we do not allow ourselves to be more aware of other selves and the bodily states that express them that we can *neither* free ourselves from them – recognising that the very awareness of them is distinct and free from them – *nor* fully affirm and body these selves as valid ways of feeling ourselves. The suffering associated with illness arises because, instead of affirming the selves we feel when we are ill, however 'foreign' they may feel to our usual sense of self, we feel 'possessed' or plagued by them - whether in the form of somatic illness or uncontrolled emotions, thoughts, inner voices or behaviours. At the same time we see the cause of such symptoms as something essentially *other than self* - whether another person, a 'malign spirit' or a 'foreign body' such as a virus, toxin or cancerous cell. Not feeling ourselves, we blame our illness on this 'other'. In this way we deprive ourselves of the opportunity to become aware of another self within us, and to both face and overcome our fears of it through that very awareness.

The Awareness Principle allows us to affirm our most elementary experience of illness as an awareness - an *awareness* of feeling our own bodies or minds as having become something 'foreign' to us, no longer fitting our previous sense of identity or self. The Medical Principle blames illness on 'foreign bodies'. Yet this is just the same as blaming the ills of society on *foreigners* – rather than seeing them as a new and healthy element of the social body, whose values can help make it more balanced and 'whole'. If we seek the causes of illness in 'foreign bodies', and seek to chemically or surgically root them out or 'eliminate' them we are acting like xenophobes or little Hitlers. Worse still, we are actively *encouraging* that which feels foreign to us – either within our own soul or within society – to take the malignant form of either illness or social ills. The Nazi state was a Medical State – one in which The Medical Principle was applied to all social problems, all of which were seen by Hitler as 'diseases' of the social 'body' or 'Volk', and blamed on racially foreign, impure or genetically unfit bodies – in particular Jews, Gypsies and the mentally or physically 'handicapped'. The 'Final Solution' to social ills was seen as a medical one – the clinical *annihilation* of all people and ideas seen as detrimental to the health of the social body. Yet like German rocket scientists, German Nazi physicians, eugenicists, psychiatrists and pharmaceutical companies played a key role in the development of *today's* 'genetic' medicine and pharmaceutical drug therapies. Nazi social 'health fascism' is reflected today in the growth of state-imposed health regulations and treatment 'regimes'. Those who seek alternative forms of healing in 'complementary' medicine on the other hand, do not realise that these are as much based on The Medical Principle and a 'Medical Model' of illness as orthodox medicine. Which is why not only vegetarianism or vehement anti-smoking campaigns, but also the promotion of exercise, herbal and homoeopathic remedies were as much a part of Nazi ideology as they are a part of today's health fads and 'health fascism'. The only *truly* alternative medicine is one whose basic principle – The Awareness Principle – challenges The Medical Principle and 'The Medical Model' of illness as such.

Healing Through Awareness 1

1. If you are feeling unwell do not think to yourself that 'you' are feeling unwell, or that 'you' are experiencing this or that physical-mental state or symptom.

2. Do not even ask *why* you are feeling the way you are, but *who* – *which you* – is feeling that way.

3. Be aware not just of what or how 'you' are feeling but how and who it makes *you* feel - the sense of self that it induces.

4. Be aware of your state of being not simply as a mental or physical state but as a distinct self or 'self-state' – a distinct *you*.

5. Remind yourself also that your current mental and physical state is but one of many 'self-states' among others, one self or *you* among many others.

6. Now identify with that self which is distinct from each and every *you* – for it is nothing but the very *awareness* of any and every self-state that can be experienced.

7. Feel this self – the *awareness self* – as a spacious field or pure centre of awareness that is absolutely *distinct* both from your current self-state or *you* and from all such self-states.

8. Choose to allow *the you* that your current state of being is bringing to the fore to *express* itself *more* fully - both in your bodily language and in your thoughts and emotions.

9. Do not try to heal or chang*e* the self or *you* that is expressing itself through your current state or symptoms but let it gradually *change* you – allowing it to alter the way you feel your self as a whole - your whole self or 'soul'.

10. Do not become 'a patient' but *be patient*. For by letting your mental-physical states and symptoms *change you* – which means feeling and expressing the *other selves* that they express – those selves will gradually no longer need to express *themselves* through states or symptoms of 'illness'.

ILLNESS
INSTEAD OF AWARENESS

AWARENESS
INSTEAD OF ILLNESS

A personal secretary finds herself stuck in a job with a bullying and abusive boss. Fearing to express her feelings of irritation, anger and embarrassed humiliation 'face to face' and 'face up to' her boss, feeling vulnerable in the face of the unpredictable rage this might unleash in her boss, and afraid with good reason that it might be 'rash' to risk her job by doing so, she keeps 'a straight face' in the face of all the bullying. Over time her feelings come to the surface in her body itself - in the form of an 'irritating' and 'angry' red skin rash. Lacking a way to face her boss, let alone 'whack him one' – even though she is itching to do so - the rash appears on her face, arms and hands. Plagued by itching, she scratches and irritates her own skin until it blisters and bleeds – an activity that provides, unaware to herself, some satisfaction in releasing her 'bad blood' towards her boss. But her feelings of embarrassment and shame about not being able to face up to her boss become displaced by shame and embarrassment about the rash itself. So she goes to her doctor. Not even thinking that asking her questions about her *life world* might have any diagnostic significance, the doctor is therefore completely blind to the metaphorical *meaning* of her

A personal secretary, faced with having to work with a bullying and abusive boss for the first time in her career, doesn't 'feel herself' at work in the way she was used to doing. She allows herself to be fully aware of her emotions of anger, vulnerability, shame and humiliation – and yet is wary of rashly letting them out in an emotional outburst that might risk her job. On a day-to-day basis she reminds herself that the awareness of an emotion, however intense is not itself an emotion or impulse but something emotion- and impulse-free. This makes her feel less vulnerable to her boss's bullying and less impelled to react emotionally to it in a rash way. Instead she sees the bullying abusiveness for what it is – as the indirect expression of a deep insecure and vulnerable self in her boss. Nevertheless, she stays with her awareness of her own emotions, allowing herself to fully affirm and feel them in her body. As a result they condense into a bodily sense of a completely different self within her, a self that feels inwardly strong enough to face up to her boss – or to anyone - and challenge them in a calm, non-reactive but nevertheless firm and resolute way. By simply letting herself feel this other self in a 'angry rash'. Applying The Medical Principle, the doctor's sole interest is in diagnosing the rash as some form of skin disorder, the 'cause' of which must for him be some impersonal 'thing' - even though there is in this case no 'thing' to explain it such as a liver disorder. Nevertheless he prescribes a cortisone cream to 'treat' and 'cure' her problem. The problem is that she then becomes dependent on the cream, which far from helping her to become tougher and more 'thick-skinned' emotionally, has the side-effect of thinning her actual skin surface itself, making it more vulnerable to embarrassing sores and bleeding. Eventually she feels forced to take more sick leave and then to leave the job altogether and seek another boss.

bodily way and give it expression through her body language and tone of voice she feels ever less vulnerable, and instead becomes even more aware of the vulnerability that lies behind her boss's bullying. Sensing this new self and awareness in her, her boss finds it strangely more difficult to be as bullying towards her as before. Now it is her boss who is uncomfortably aware of feeling another self, a less powerful and more vulnerable self. Afraid of this self, her boss reacts by actively intensifying the abusive bullying, only to find it met by a calm, resolute and firmly toned response from the secretary. Yet her boss now feels so secretly ashamed of bullying the secretary that she is not fired. She does not develop a rash, feels ready to face up to bullying, and as a result does not feel vulnerable, shamed or humiliated.

Illness as an Awareness

Every feeling, symptom, mental or physical state, together with our overall sense of self or 'self-state' is not just something we are aware *of*. Its meaning lies in the fact that *it is itself an awareness* of something. Thus a head or neck ache, though we aware *of* it as a bodily tension itself *embodies an awareness* of something beyond it – for example an awareness of real personal tensions in our lives, relationships or place of work.

Just as a person whose family has been made homeless or wiped out in a war has *good reasons* for feeling 'depressed', so do all feelings – including feeling 'depressed', 'anxious', 'angry' or 'ill' – have good reasons. They are not just programmed or mechanical physiological reactions to or 'effects' of external or internal 'causes'. Simply to label feelings as 'positive' or 'negative', to describe ourselves as 'well' or 'unwell', or to call the way we feel as 'good' or 'bad', is to deny the inherent *meaning* of all feelings - as an awareness of something beyond themselves. Symptoms of illness, like dream symbols, are a form of *condensed* awareness. Their *inherently* positive value and meaning lies in helping us to become more *directly* aware of what it is that they themselves *are* a condensed or embodied awareness of. Thus digestive problems are a condensed embodied awareness of an aspect of our lives or lived experience of the world we find difficult to 'stomach' or 'digest'.

Even though illness is often or mainly experienced through *localised* bodily symptoms (including 'mental' states such as a sense of confusion localised in our heads), every such symptom is also and always accompanied by a state of consciousness or 'mood' that pervades *our entire body* and in this way also affects our entire *bodily sense of self.* This bodily sense of self or 'self-state' is itself an undifferentiated *awareness* of what may be many different aspects of our overall *life world* that are difficult or uncomfortable, distressing or disturbing for us - thus giving rise to a general sense of 'dis-ease'. That is why, in order to find meaning in the overall bodily sense of 'unwellness' or 'dis-ease' that accompanies a specific illness, it is necessary first to experience it *as* a *self-state* – to be aware of how it imparts an overall colour, mood and texture to our bodily sense of self, one which in turn colours our experience of our whole *life world*. To pass from an experience of illness as 'not feeling ourselves' to one of 'feeling another self' – a distinct self or 'self-state' – means experiencing this distinct bodily sense of self. The 'other self' we experience through illness however is, by definition, *an experienced self* – a self we are aware *of*. Our self as a whole or 'soul' on the other hand, is not essentially any *experienced* self, symptom, state of consciousness or 'self-state', but rather the very *awareness* of experiencing it. To avoid becoming unconsciously identified with the self-states and symptoms of dis-ease, it is necessary to identify with that 'whole self' which is nothing *but* this awareness – the *experiencing self* rather than any *experienced self*. Only within the awareness that *is* this self – our 'awareness self' – can we in turn feel and affirm every particular feeling and self we experience or are aware *of*. We are as much aware of our *self as a whole* – our soul – as we are aware of our *body* as a whole. Yet the 'body' of our whole self or soul – our *awareness self* – is not just our physical body but *our entire life world*. For, it is an awareness that embraces everything and 'every-body' in our world, from our immediate present reality and relationships to our past and future – and ultimately the entire universe.

The *second* step in healing ourselves through awareness is therefore to experience each and every localised bodily sensation or symptom, no matter how subtle, *as* an *awareness* of some specific aspect of our larger body – of our life world. Thus by giving more awareness to a localised muscular tension we can experience it *as* an awareness of a specific tension in our life world. Through a meditational process of giving awareness to each and every *localised* bodily feeling or sensation of dis-ease – no matter how subtle, and by making sure we attend to each and every *region* of our body in the process – we can come to experience each of these feelings and sensations *as* an awareness of

120

some aspect of our larger body or life world. Through this process we are literally putting ourselves together – 're-membering' and making whole that larger body that is our life world *as a whole*. And by simply *granting* awareness to each region of our bodies and each sensation or feeling of dis-ease or discomfort we experience within it, our overall sense of dis-ease and overall 'self-state' will automatically begin to alter. For we will feel ever-more pervaded, lightened and healed by that very self which is the *awareness* we grant – both to our overall self-state *and* to the specific, localised feelings and sensations it unites – that 'whole self' which *is* nothing but the pure, healing light of *awareness as such*, one which pervades the entire universe and every body in it.

Healing through Awareness 2

1. Give yourself time to attend to your immediate bodily sense of any discomfort, tension or emotional feeling - however intense or delicate and subtle – that you are aware of. Be more aware of where and how you feel it in your body.

2. Staying aware of any such localised sensation or feeling of dis-ease, remind yourself that it is itself an awareness of some aspect of your life-world and relationships that is a source of unease or 'dis-ease'.

3. Wait until a spontaneous awareness arises of what specific aspect of your life-world it is that the sensation or feeling of dis-ease embodies.

4. Grant awareness to one localised sensation or feeling of dis-ease or discomfort after another, staying with it long enough until it too recalls you to some specific aspect of your life world, present, past or future.

5. Take time to follow this process through – making sure you attend to every region of your body *in* the process – until your *overall* sense of dis-ease lifts and your overall sense of your self and body alters - feeling lightened and pervaded by the very awareness you are granting it.

The Body as a Language of Awareness

When we speak of someone 'losing heart', feeling 'disheartened' or 'heart-broken' we are not just using the language of a biological 'organ' – in this case the heart – as a metaphor for a psychological state of 'dis-ease'. It is the other way round. Heart disease is itself *a living biological metaphor* of psychic states of dis-ease such as feeling 'heart-broken', 'heartless' or 'cold-hearted'. Similarly, respiratory disorders such as asthma arise from feeling 'stifled' or 'having no room to breathe', and digestive disorders from aspects of our lives we do not feel able to 'stomach' or 'digest' in our awareness. The 'body language' used in phrases such as 'hard to stomach' in other words, are not 'mere' mental metaphors. Instead they point in a quite literal way to incapacities or states of dis-ease belonging to our subjectively felt body or *psychical body* – and how these in turn can find metaphorical expression in organic diseases and dysfunctions of our *physical body.*

The Medical Principle seeks 'organic' causes for illness in dysfunctions of our *biological organs*, and sees even psychical states and disorders as the result of such organic dysfunctions. As a result, medicine is blind to the deeper meaning and truth of the bodily 'metaphors' we use to describe psychical feelings and states – which are a way of recognising that the physical body and its biological organs are themselves a *living metaphorical language* of the soul or psyche – of awareness. In contrast to The Medical Principle, The Awareness Principle recognises all physical body organs and their functions as biological embodiments of our psychic body and psychical capacities. The human psychical body or 'soul body' is our awareness body – that body with which we breathe, stomach, digest, absorb and let circulate and give physical expression to our *awareness* of all we experience.

Biological organs such as lungs, stomach and heart and their corresponding *physiological functions* are localised biological expressions of these *psychical capacitie*s, which are essentially *capacities of awareness.* It is the absence or dysfunctioning of these *capacities* of awareness – for example our capacity to breathe, digest, metabolise, absorb, let circulate and give expression to awareness in muscular activity – that finds metaphorical expression in 'organic', biological dysfunctions, not the other way round. It is these psychic capacities of awareness that find living biological expression in our physical body organs and organic 'functions' such as respiration, digestion and circulation, just as it is psychic incapacities that find expression in organic, biological dysfunctions or disorders. In other words, it is not illness that *incapacitates* us. Instead it is failure to fully or properly exercise our *psychical capacities* – awareness – that results in incapacitating illness.

Our *biology* has its basis in our *biography*, and in that larger *body of awareness* that is our *life world* as a whole. For it is always within the specific contexts of our life world that we experience 'dis-ease', just as it is *capacities of awareness* that allow us to relate to and respond to our life world in a healthy way – *with* awareness.

Illness can and has been understood in many ways: in a purely objective and biomedical way, as a mechanical neuro-physiological 'effect' of psychical stress or trauma, as a relation to our life world and other people in it, as a form of silent bodily *communication* or even protest, as blocked action or communication, and/or as a metaphorical *language* through which we give silent bodily *expression* to any *subjectively* felt 'dis-ease'. Understanding illness as a metaphorical *language of awareness* embraces all other understandings of it. More importantly it provides us with an understanding of illness that affirms its innate *meaningfulness* in the life of the individual – as an expression and embodiment of their lived experience of themselves and of their life world as a whole, as an expression and embodiment of the degree of awareness they bring to their experience, and as an expression and embodiment too, of the specific capacities or 'organs' of awareness that they do or do not exercise in relating and responding to their experienced self and world – for it is these specific capacities that offer new keys to diagnosing illness *as* a 'language of awareness'.

Counselling, Meditation and Yoga

What is 'meditation'? And is there such a thing as a 'yogic' or 'meditational' approach to both counselling and psychotherapy?

The term 'Non-Dual Therapy' has now established itself as a type of umbrella term for approaches to counselling and therapy rooted in yogic philosophy and incorporating both a spiritual or 'trans-personal' dimension and meditational practices of different sorts.

First a word about words and terms. The term 'meditation', though it is of course associated with Eastern spiritual traditions, is not itself an Eastern word but a European one. It derives from the Latin words *mederi* (to give attention or awareness to something or someone) and *meditari* (to reflect, study on or apply oneself to something). It is commonly used to translate the Sanskrit term *Sadhana* – meaning 'to practice'.

The expression 'non-dual' is a direct and literal translation of the Sanskrit term *Advaita*. 'Non-duality' or *Advaita* are terms closely related in meaning with the word 'yoga' itself - which means 'union' and derives from the Indo-European root *ieug* (to join or yoke together).

Advaita or 'non-dualism' (*A-dvaita*) is also the name and the basic principle of an important school of Indian 'yogic' philosophy, aimed at distinguishing it from so-called 'dualistic' or *Dvaita* schools. It is this basic principle that I have rethought, refined and redefined - calling it simply 'The Awareness Principle'.

What is the essence of 'non-duality' (*Advaita*) or 'union' (*yoga*)? In my understanding it is not just 'one-ness' as opposed to duality or 'two-ness', 'union' as opposed to separation – for this would constitute a *dualistic* opposition in itself. Instead the essence of both 'union' and 'non-duality' can best be seen as a relation of *inseparable distinction*. An example is the relation between two sides of the same coin or sheet of paper – which are both distinct (and therefore dual) but also absolutely inseparable (and therefore non-dual).

In the development of Advaitic or non-dual philosophy itself, it was acknowledged that to see non-duality and duality as opposing or *dual* concepts would run against the very principle of *non*-duality. Only a new understanding of unity or non-duality as a relation of 'inseparable distinction' can fully clarify what, in the *Advaitic* tradition itself, was called 'the non-duality of duality and non-duality'.

Another example of 'non-duality' as 'inseparable distinction' is the relation of empty space to the objects in it. For space is both inseparable from everything in it and yet at the same time distinct from it.

Yet what have these abstract philosophical terms and concepts to do with counselling? The most important thing to understand is that, unlike yogic practices and the philosophy of non-dualism, no Western *psychology* or form of counselling has any concept of a type of *pure awareness* which – like space – is both inseparable and yet absolutely distinct from everything we experience within it – whether outer perceptions, or inwardly experienced moods and sensations, needs and impulses, thoughts and emotions.

The Western 'psychological' understanding (and experience) of the soul or *psyche* is a sort of internal space of awareness inside our head or bodies and bounded by them. Yet most people neither sense the insideness of their bodies nor the space around them as a space of clear uncluttered awareness. Instead they may either feel 'empty' in a depressed way, or else as brimful of impulses and sensations, thoughts and emotions, voices and mental images, memories, impulses and other elements of experience to the point of 'overwhelm'. It is such elements of their experiencing which so pre-occupy the *space* of people's inner and outer worlds that they derive their whole sense of *self* from them –

whilst at the same time leaving them quite literally with a sense of having no 'space' for themselves or for significant others.

The aim of *Advaitic* philosophy and yogic meditational practice is to find that space and in doing so feel a quite different self to the one that has 'no space' for itself or others. This is a self that is able to feel *space itself* as a realm of pure awareness distinct and free from anything experienced within it.

This self is not the everyday personal self we are aware of. It is not even a self that can be said to 'have' or 'possess' awareness. Instead it is that Self which *is* awareness. The idea of a Self that is identical with awareness *as such* is not my invention. For one of the important yogic treatise or *tantra* – the 'Shiva Sutras'– declares as its opening statement or sutra that 'Awareness *is* the Self'.

This Self, which I term 'The Awareness Self', was called *Atman, Chaitanya* or *Chaitanyatman.* It was understood as 'non-dual' – as inseparable from a universal soul or ultimate and divine awareness (*Anuttara*). Identifying with *this* Self was understood as a way of freeing or liberating ourselves from identification with a much more limited self – that self which is wholly identified or bound up with whatever is currently going on, whatever we are currently doing or saying, whatever we are currently focussing our awareness on - or whatever is preoccupying the inner and outer spaces of our awareness. That is why in another famous treatise – the Vijnanabhairava Tantra – identification with the apparent emptiness of space was seen as a key to the ultimate aim of yoga – freedom or *Moksha.* By this was meant freedom from a self-limiting identification with anything we happen to be experiencing or aware *of.*

Now this distinction between a liberated or unbound self and a bound or limited self, between that self which *is* awareness and any self we are aware *of* – has profound significance in the context of counselling and therapy. Why? Because whilst the aim of counselling is to help people get 'clearer' about

126

troubling experiences and emotions, and in this way to also 'free' them from them, the aim is a difficult if not impossible one to achieve if a client's whole *sense of self* is identified and bound up with their suffering – if not wholly dependent on it.

The vital role that yoga has to play in counselling is to show how it is possible to identify and achieve union with the 'Awareness Self' – that self which does not 'have' but *is* awareness.

Learning to identify with space itself, inner and outer, as pure awareness and thereby uniting with that Self which is awareness – this is 'yoga' in the truest sense. At its heart is what I term 'The Awareness Principle', which together with the many 'Practices of Awareness' that go with it, constitute what I call 'The New Yoga of Awareness'.

Teaching this New Yoga to counselling clients requires first of all that counsellors themselves learn what is perhaps the most basic Principle and Practice of Awareness. This is the principle and practice of distinguishing between each and every thing we are *aware of* (whether within or around us, positive or negative, painful or pleasurable) from the *pure awareness* of it – from awareness *as such*.

To engage in this Practice of Awareness it is helpful, if not vital, to remind ourselves of the basic relation between pure awareness and 'empty' space. A simple way of helping someone to understand this relation is to request that they look around and name any tangible thing they are aware of around them – a wall painting, computer, chair or desk for example – and then to put to them the following simple questions: "Is *the awareness* of that thing itself a 'thing' of any sort?" For example: "Is *the awareness* of a painting, computer, desk or chair *itself* a painting, computer, desk or chair?"

The point that such questions can help to get over is that *awareness* of an object in the space around us is not itself an object 'in' space. Instead awareness *is* the very space in which any object is perceived. Your outer awareness of a table for example is not *itself* a table, but the space in which you perceive it. Similarly, the inner awareness of a sensation, thought or emotion is *not itself* a sensation, thought or emotion. Instead it is the inner *space* within which the sensation, thought or emotion is experienced. The same basic Principle of Awareness in other words, applies to any and all 'elements' of our experience, inner and outer – showing that awareness *as such* is distinct from all of them.

Since the awareness of a thought, for example, *is not itself a thought*, awareness as such is something innately *thought-free* – just as it is also innately free of each and every element of our experience.

Consequently – and yet in contrast to how many actual or would-be practitioners of meditation see it – to achieve a meditative state of pure 'thought-free' awareness does not require any effort at all; does not require us to 'clear' or 'free' our minds of thoughts. All that is required is to identify with the already clear and thought-free space of awareness *within which* we experience any thought.

Coming to rest within a space of pure awareness is the essence of *meditation*. That is why 'meditation' – as long as it is clearly understood as a practice of *awareness* and not merely a practice of walking or sitting in a certain way - is the central link between counselling and yoga. Yet though the terms 'meditation' and 'yoga' are commonly used, their meaning is rarely considered or defined in such precise way. Only in this way however, can their value for counsellors and their clients become apparent.

In what I call 'The New Yoga' – the yoga of *awareness* – 'yoga' does not mean sitting alone or in class with people and effortfully adopting different bodily postures or engaging in stretching exercises. Nor does 'meditation' mean effortfully attempting to empty your mind in expectation of some undefined state of 'enlightenment'. It is not 'just sitting' but 'just being aware' – sitting with the simple intent to give ourselves *time to be aware*. Giving ourselves *time* to be aware allows us to become much *more* aware than we usually are of all that is going on within and around us. This in turn allows us to do three important things:

Firstly, it allows us to *identify and distinguish* much more clearly all the different elements of our immediate experiencing such as moods, sensations, memories, thoughts emotions etc.

Secondly it allow us to *fully acknowledge, feel and affirm* each and every element of our immediate experiencing – whether pleasurable or painful, mental, emotional or somatic.

Last but not least, it allows us to distinguish each and every element of our current experience from the pure awareness of it, and to feel that very awareness as a clear space in which we can feel independent and free of anything we experience or are aware of.

Sometimes people confuse dis-identification with 'detaching' ourselves from our feelings and other elements of our experience. This is a misunderstanding. For meditation begins with freely choosing to *feel* our feelings - and all elements of our experience - more fully and not less. To *feel and affirm* a particular mood, sensation, desire, emotion or thought is by no means the same thing as *identifying* with that element of our experience. Indeed it is the very opposite of doing so. For freely choosing to become more aware of something is itself the very first step to identifying with pure awareness as such. And it is by giving ourselves time to feel and follow any element of our experience that it will transform – revealing itself to *be an awareness* of something beyond it. A sensation, emotion or thought for example, is not only something we are aware *of*. It is itself the expression *of* an awareness, for example in the form of a new insight into a particular situation, possibility or person.

To follow our experiences to this point of transformation, as well as reaching a state of identification with *pure awareness* takes time however, which is why the defining principle and practice of meditation – giving ourselves *time* to be aware – is so important.

For we know also that in today's globalised Western culture people are driven to occupy their time with everything *but* awareness – to keep themselves permanently preoccupied and busy with different activities. The result of this culture of busy-ness is that people keep their awareness so filled up and preoccupied that they end up feeling no space for themselves – or no self to feel. This in turn makes them more addicted to activities, mental-emotional states, behaviours or experiences which – whether habitual or compulsive, mundane or 'extreme', pleasurable or painful, normal or pathological – can serve to bestow or restore a sense of self.

It is significant too, that in everyday English – itself a global language – the phrases 'don't have time for' and 'don't have space for...' or 'wish I had more time for..' and 'wish I had more space for...' are used synonymously. This not having space for things or people – not to mention oneself – comes about through not meditating, through not giving ourselves *time* to just be aware. Conversely however, giving ourselves that time to be aware is what gives us a sense of having more *space*.

This brings us to another reason why people would rather *not* give themselves time to be aware – and instead see even such things as counselling, meditation and yoga as just other thing to 'do' or 'experience', other ways of 'using' or 'filling' time. The reason I refer to is *fear* – the fear that if they did truly meditate, if they *did* give themselves more time to be aware and *did* feel more space as a result, they might feel that space as totally empty – a black hole, void or vacuum devoid of any self at all, rather than as a space of pure, liberating awareness. For this is a space distinct from all the things that normally preoccupy us and yet expansive enough to embrace them in such a way that we no longer feel stressed or overwhelmed by them. It is a space in which we can feel even our ordinary limited experience of ourselves safely held - yet one that is at the same time big enough to 'make room' for others - and for *new* experiences of ourselves and the world around us. 'Meditation' means entering this expanded *space* of awareness by giving ourselves more *time* to be aware.

Many people have been introduced to or practiced different forms of 'meditation'. What follows is a description of some basic stages of meditation based on the precise definition of it given above – as a practice of giving ourselves *time to be aware* and in this way expanding the *space* of awareness in which we can dwell – not just whilst meditating but throughout our everyday lives.

1. To begin with, take time to look around and become more aware of the different elements of your *outer experiencing* – for example the different features of the people and objects in this room. Now take time to be aware of the clear space surrounding everything and everybody in this room, not just the space you can see in front of you but the space as you can sense it both in front of you and behind you, above you and to either side of you. Sense this clear space not just as an empty space surrounding the things and people you are aware of but as a clear space *of* awareness, one without which you could not be aware of anything or anybody within it.

2. The next stage is to close your eyes, turn your gaze inwards with your inner eye and take time to be more aware of the different elements of your inner

experiencing. To begin with, just sense the interiority or insideness of different regions of your body – whether head, chest, belly or abdomen. Sense each of these regions of your body as if it were a hollow space. If you can, feel these hollow spaces of head, chest, belly and abdomen as one singular space or hollow of awareness bounded by your body.

Now take two or three minutes to become *more aware*, one by one, of the different types of thing you can sense yourself experiencing within these spaces – for example the tone and 'colour' of your overall mood, subtle bodily sensations and tensions, thoughts and feelings about your yourself and others etc. Allow yourself also to be aware, in the present, of thoughts and feelings arising from recollections of recent events and experiences or anticipations of future ones. Most importantly, if you are or become aware of any sense of dis-ease, of any discomforting thoughts, feelings or sensations, do all of the following three things:

- Firstly give them more awareness – all the awareness they are asking for.
- Secondly, remind yourself that the very awareness of a thought, feeling or sensation is not itself a thought, feeling or sensation.
- Thirdly, whenever you sense yourself identifying with any discomforting thoughts, feelings or sensation, remind yourself to identify instead with the space or spaces of awareness within which you experience them.

3. The third stage of this introductory meditation or introduction to meditation – slowly open your eyes again. Yet as you once again become more aware of the space of this room surrounding your body, stay aware of the inner space or spaces of awareness within your body and of what you are aware of within it. Finally, begin to feel the outer space around your body and the inner spaces

within it as non-different or non-dual – as one singular space of pure awareness that extends from an infinite inwardness within your body to the outermost boundaries of the cosmos. Feel this singular space of awareness pervading and vitalising the spaces within every atom and cell of your body.

If, having studied and practiced these stages of meditation, you may find some of the questions below helpful in reviewing your experience of it:

- What sort of things did you become aware of in the space of this room? How did it feel to sense and identify with the space itself and feel it as a field of awareness?

- What sort of things did you become aware of in the felt hollows of your body? How did it feel to give discomforting things more awareness and then identify more with the spaces of awareness in which you felt them?

- What was it like to open your eyes again, be aware of the space around you and yet stay aware of the inner spaces of your body and what you were aware of there?

- What was it like to feel the spaces around and within as one singular, non-dual and unbounded space of pure awareness?

With the new understandings of yoga and meditation presented so far in this essay, let us now return to the question of their relation to counselling. As counsellors or therapists we want our clients to feel safe enough with us to 'open up' – to share things they are aware of. Yet if, like most people, they experience their awareness as a space closed off and bounded by their own bodies - or even just enclosed in their own heads – then surely the first step in counselling and therapy is to help them to open up and expand that very space. For only in this way can they feel it as a space safe enough to share from - which means big enough to easily embrace all that they experience and go through, and with room left over, room big enough to let in other people, to let in new insights and a whole new sense of self.

As counsellors or therapists we also seek to create in our consulting rooms a 'safe space' – a so-called 'holding space' in which people can freely and honestly share their feelings. But if both counsellor and client experience their awareness as something enclosed by their bodies, neither the smallest nor the biggest counselling or therapy room in the world can be actually felt as a safely holding space of awareness – one in which both client and counsellor can feel 'held', and in which both can come to fully let in and embrace each other.

For an awareness-based or yogic counsellor – a practitioner of awareness or 'yogi' – it just needs a single glance at a person's body to see how physically closed or open, enclosed or 'wrapped up' their consciousness is in themselves – how aware or unaware they are of the field or space of awareness around their bodies and the things and people in it, and how narrow or spacious the 'inner space' of awareness is that they can sense and hold open within their bodies.

That is because yoga is not just about the twin realms of mental and emotional experiencing that counselling and psychotherapy focus on. Instead it recognises a *third realm* – that of the senses and of immediate *sensory* experiencing – as more inclusive and fundamental.

Only by cultivating a direct *sensory* experience of emotions in our bodies and a direct sensory experience of mental states in our heads can we stop our thoughts and emotions just feeding off and reinforcing one another in vicious circles. Yet it is surprising how difficult people can find it to get their heads around the thought that *thoughts themselves* can by directly sensed in awareness - for example as mental images, by hearing them as mental words or speech in our minds, or by sensing in our bodies the way they affect our emotions – just as emotions can be directly felt as bodily sensations. To be truly aware of our mental-emotional or somatic states rather than getting wrapped up in them, the first step must be to attend to the qualities belonging to our immediate *sensory* experience of them.

The fact that certain clients may be less willing or find it less satisfactory than others to talk 'about' their mental-emotional states (not least those suffering acute stress or showing signs of so-called borderline and psychotic states) has a good reason. My belief is that for such clients (indeed for all clients if not for all people) what they unknowingly want most of all from another is someone who – like a mother – will take time to first of all give full sensory awareness to their *body*. For only in this way can they feel that their own wordless, bodily sense *of* 'how they are feeling' is being sensed and felt by another – rather than forced into words. For the language, by its very nature, distances our awareness from our immediate sensory experience of our own self, body and state of being.

It is only relatively recently that terms such as 'bodily sensing' and 'somatic resonance' have been coined to refer to this type of direct *sensory* 'empathy' for another person's mental and emotional states. The need to which these terms respond is not just a need to be looked at and listened to in an emotionally sensitive or caring way. Still less is it a need to be drawn out into discussions 'about' one's thoughts and feelings. Instead it is the primordial need to feel one's whole body sensed and embraced by another within the space of an all-round, womb-like space of awareness.

It is the sensory awareness given by the counsellor to the *body* of the client and what it shows, and the all-round spatial *embrace* of this awareness, that helps clients to *feel safer* in their bodies and to get closer to their own sensory experience of themselves – rather than distancing themselves from it through words and talk 'about'. It also helps clients to apply The Awareness Principle themselves, to embrace their own sensory experience of themselves – however stressed or distressing – in a safe and expanded space of awareness.

The emphasis on giving awareness primarily to our immediate sensory experiencing is another important difference, derived from the tantric tradition, between yoga and meditation on the one hand, and psychology and counselling on the other.

A further and most fundamental difference is that yoga and meditation, unlike psychology and counselling, are not merely 'person-centred' – focussed on the personal or inter-personal dimensions of awareness and experience.

For a basic precept of The Awareness Principle is the recognition of the fundamentally *non-individual* or *trans-personal* nature of the awareness within which all personal and inter-personal experiencing occurs. For though people speak casually of 'self-awareness' in connection with 'counselling' and of personal or spiritual 'growth', the deeper truth is that awareness of self cannot – *in principle* – be the private property of any person or self we are *aware of*.

Awareness, in other words, is not essentially 'yours' or 'mine', 'his' or 'hers'. On the contrary, every person's individual sense of 'me-ness' or 'self' is an individualised expression and embodiment of a non-individuated and trans-personal awareness – that ultimate and universal awareness that Indian thought identifies with the Divine, with 'God' or 'God-consciousness'.

One important reason why Indian philosophy is ignored in Western psychology is that it challenges the privatisation of the psyche in Western culture – the reduction of awareness to the private property of persons or a mere biological function of their bodies and brains. As a result, psychological problems suffered by individuals are also privatised – seen as 'their' problem rather than as an expression of a culture which denies any higher, trans-personal or divine dimensions to awareness. In this culture people are *indoctrinated* into believing that consciousness is something bounded by their bodies and a product of their brains. Psychiatry is the pseudo-science founded on this crude biologistic doctrine – which serves nothing but the profits of the pharmaceutical corporations – and replaces meditation with damagingly awareness-numbing *medication*. The idea that this shallowest of modern doctrines is truer or more 'scientific' than the profound metaphysical understandings of the soul articulated and preserved in Eastern yogic philosophies and practices for millennia is arrogant to say the least.

All the more pity then, that what passes as 'yoga' in the West today has become a mere crass commercialisation and commodification of bodily stretching exercises that have nothing to do with awareness at all, let alone with 'non-dual' awareness.

Taking the word 'yoga' in its root meaning of 'union' - to 'yoke' or 'conjoin' – we can now understand it as a practice of awareness designed to unite our everyday self, the 'experienced self', with another Self, the 'experiencing self'. This experiencing self is nothing but the Awareness Self, that Self which does not 'have' or 'possess' awareness but *is* awareness – an awareness inseparable from that unbounded, absolute, ultimate and universal awareness that Indian thought recognised as the essence of the Divine.

Such metaphysical and spiritual dimensions of awareness cannot be confined to the realm of Eastern spiritual philosophies and traditions however. For they are profoundly relevant to both everyday life and to the theory and practice of counselling. This is because they offer answers to basic questions concerning the essential nature of the self. Yet both the answers and the questions are of a sort which Western psychology and psychiatry continue to ignore, deny or marginalise - blinded as they are by the delusion that awareness is the private property of persons, bounded by the body and a product of the brain. As a result, an individual's mental, emotional or behavioural 'symptoms' are seen merely as diagnostic signs of different categories of 'mental illness' – rather than as *invitations and opportunities* for the sufferer to give themselves more *awareness*.

One final remark is necessary in this context. The Buddhist term 'mindfulness' has now been co-opted into the language of Western psychology and counselling, both in the form 'Mindfulness Based Cognitive Therapy' and as part of what is called 'Dialectical Behaviour Therapy'. The term 'mindfulness' however (actually a mis-translation of the Sanskrit word for 'memory') is a wholly *imprecise and inappropriate substitute* for the word 'awareness', implying as it does that the 'mind' can in some way be aware of or monitor itself, and that awareness itself is a mere mental state or some form of mental activity. It is not. For whilst pure awareness *embraces* all mental states and activities, it is not itself a mental state or activity – or indeed any activity at all – let alone a function of 'mind' (Sanskrit *Buddhi*). It is awareness and not 'mind' or 'mindfulness' that is the key to the relation between Counselling, Meditation and Yoga.

Awareness-Based Cognitive Therapy

Awareness-Based Cognitive Therapy (ABCT) applies The Awareness Principle and The Practice of Awareness to counselling, psychotherapy and medical practice. In contrast to other forms of therapy - including other 'cognitive' therapies – its focus does not lie on *specific contents of the client's consciousness* or *specific elements of their experience* (event, thoughts, feelings etc) or their relation, but rather on a Fundamental Distinction between *all* such contents – all elements of our experience - and the larger space or 'field' of awareness in which they arise.

Who can benefit from ABCT?

Counsellors, life coaches and psychotherapists, physicians and other medical and psychiatric professionals, social workers and carers, managers, teachers and parents, alternative health practitioners – and all those seeking aid or care from them.

How can they benefit?

1. By learning to be fully aware of and open to their own subjective experience and emotions and those of individuals in their care, but ...

    o   **Without** being overwhelmed by them.
    o   **Without** feeling them as a source of constant 'stress'.
    o   **Without** having to shut out or act out, suppress or somatise their experience.
    o   **Without** having to hide themselves behind a professional mask, role or persona.
    o   **Without** having to clinically objectify or label another person's distress or dis-ease.
    o   **Instead** being open to and able to respond to any experience, person or situation in an aware, free and non-reactive way.

2. By showing those seeking their aid or care how they also can be fully aware of and open to their own subjective experience of themselves and others, but …

- o **Without** being overwhelmed by their experience.
- o **Without** thinking there is something 'wrong' with them.
- o **Without** identifying with their experience and reacting from it.
- o **Without** having to shut out or act out, suppress or somatise their experience.
- o **Without** having to identify with medical labels and/or with the roles of bad, mad, sick or 'difficult' people.
- o **Instead** having a direct feeling awareness of the innate meaningfulness of their experience and behaviour, transforming it through this awareness.

Whenever a new therapeutic principle or practice is announced, the key questions asked about it in today's economically governed world are:

- whether it is *effective?*

- whether it is *economic?*

- whether it is *'evidence-based'* and therefore 'scientific'?

The final question is the most fundamental one in relation to the first two, for it rests on an unquestioned concept of 'science' itself. This concept in turn has lead to counter-productive notions of 'effectiveness' and 'economy' based solely on so-called 'objective' criteria – those that can be reduced to measurable quantities. The basic presuppositions of the dominant Western conception of science are not themselves the object of any possible scientific experiment. The Awareness Principle is a new *scientific* as well as therapeutic principle because it challenges these presuppositions in the most evidential or empirical way possible – in a way more 'scientific' than science itself. It does so by recognising that the first, most self-evidential, experiential, 'empirical' or 'scientific' fact is *not* the objective existence of a universe of things but *subjective awareness* of that universe. That awareness however, is not itself any sort of thing or object – and therefore cannot, in principle, be explained by or reduced to any thing or things we are aware of. The most basic presupposition of science is that it identifies reality with *objectivity*. The Awareness Principle reasserts the primary, universal reality of *subjectivity* – of awareness.

Again, most forms of counselling and psychotherapy - including various forms of Cognitive Therapy – take as their starting point specific elements of the client's experience or 'contents' of consciousness – whether life situations or events, thoughts about them, emotions or body sensations, dream symbols or somatic symptoms, reactive or 'maladaptive' behaviours. They then seek to link these, intuitively or 'scientifically' in chains of 'causes' and 'effects' (Diagram 1). Even if multiple causal 'factors' or reciprocal relationships between different elements are admitted, the model remains based only on *linear* relations between elements. Other models (Diagram 2) see the different elements of our experience as part of a structured whole, a 'complex' or 'gestalt' that is more than the sum of its parts.

Diagram 1   **Diagram 2**

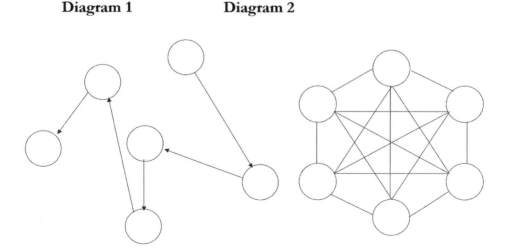

141

Both models reduce the individual soul or psyche to elements of the individual's experience, whether linked in causal chains or seen as structures or complexes of interrelated elements. Both models – and the approaches to counselling and therapy deriving from them – also ignore the larger background field of *awareness* (hatched area in Diagram 3) from and within which *all* elements of our experience emerge.

Diagram 3

elements of *experience*

field of *awareness*

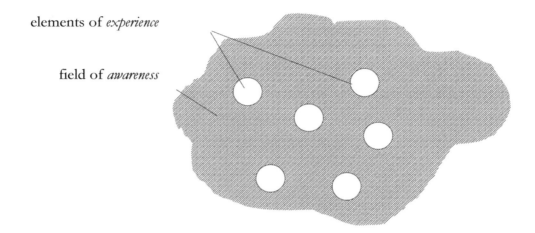

The more we *focus* awareness on any given element(s) of our experience however, the less sense we have of the larger background *field* of awareness within which alone they stand out or 'ex-ist'. Yet it is only from and *as* this awareness field – which is present not only around but *within* each of its elements – that we can *feel* ourselves into these elements. It is in this way that we can gain a true *inner* sense of each element and of their *inner* connection.

That is why Awareness Based Cognitive Therapy is based on a 'Fundamental Distinction' – the distinction between all such contents of consciousness and elements of experience – every possible thing we are aware of – and *awareness as such*. Instead of encouraging the client to focus awareness on *localised contents* of *consciousness* or *specific elements of experience* such as body

142

sensations, thoughts or emotions and to turn these into clinical 'objects' of analysis and manipulation, the aim of ABCT is to help the client to experience the essentially non-local or 'field' character of awareness – and the inherent freeing and therapeutic effect of identifying with this 'meta-cognitive', 'transcendental' or *field awareness*. The aims of ABCT are achieved on the basis of the following 'four recognitions':

1. Recognition of **The Fundamental Distinction** - between awareness as such and specific things we are aware of (contents of consciousness).
2. Recognition that awareness, like space, *transcends* all we perceive or experience within it.
3. Recognition of **The Fundamental Choice** - between identifying with things we experience, or identifying with the spacious *awareness field* in which we experience them.
4. Recognition that awareness is not only 'transcendent' but 'immanent' – present within all things, and that therefore anything we are aware of, including thoughts, emotions, sensations or symptoms of dis-ease, is *itself* an awareness.

These four recognitions allow the client to practice the **Basic Awareness Cycle**:

1. **Being Aware** of all there is to be aware of. This needs time. Giving ourselves the necessary time to be more aware of things and aware of more things is the common essence of both therapy and meditation.
2. **Bodying Awareness** – not verbally labelling the things we are aware of but giving ourselves time to be aware of our bodies and of our wordless bodily awareness of things.
3. **Being Awareness** – giving ourselves time to distinguish anything we are aware of from the very awareness of it – and identifying with or 'being' that awareness itself.
4. **Being the Awareness that things themselves are** – giving ourselves time to feel what any 'thing' we are aware of (for example a mood, body sensation or symptom) is itself a (hidden or indirect) awareness of. In this way we no longer experience the thing as a thing at all but as an awareness of something or someone else beyond it – thus returning us to step 1 in the awareness cycle (**Being Aware**).

'Being Awareness' means identifying with the 'spaces' of awareness, inner or outer, in which we experience things - within which each and every element of our experience emerges and takes shape. This means stepping back into *field awareness* rather than seeking some external and 'objective' vantage point from which to focus on the different elements of our experience. In reality no such 'objective' vantage point is possible. That is because all possible vantage points - for example thoughts about our experience or theoretical models of it – are themselves *part of* our experience and nothing separate or *apart from* it. They too emerge from and take shape within that larger space or field of awareness which is the true essence of the 'soul' or 'psyche' – not its elements or contents – even though this field of awareness is in turn coloured and toned by each of the elements within it. Focal awareness narrows our awareness field. The more bounded and contracted our awareness field becomes however (see bounded area in Diagram 4) the less elements of our experience we are aware of.

Diagram 4

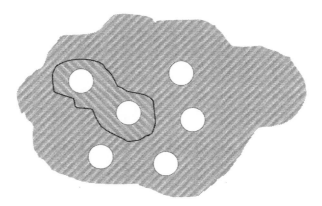

If we identify with the spacious *field* dimension of awareness on the other hand, we not only embrace more elements of our actual experience in awareness, but also create space to allow hitherto hidden or latent elements of our experience (grey-shaded circles in Diagram 5) to come into awareness.

144

Diagram 5

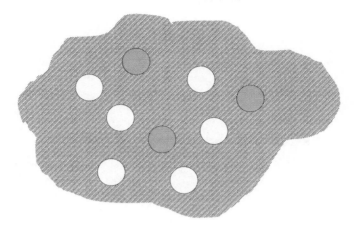

The principal purpose of training in ABCT is to provide an effective understanding and experience of the Awareness Principle and its Practice as a precisely sequenced series of awareness-raising questions and exercises designed to first of all cultivate whole-body awareness and then to experience 'pure' awareness in its fundamental character – as the very space (inner or outer) in which we become aware of things. For the *relation* between awareness as such and different things we are aware of is not only 'analogous' to the relation between the seeming emptiness of space on the one hand and sensory objects in space on the other – it IS that relation. A basic message of the course is that space as such is not essentially an 'objective' dimension of the 'physical' reality, but a basic dimension of subjectivity or awareness itself – that which allows both things and thoughts to emerge (Greek 'physis') into or stand out ('ex-ist') in awareness.

Basic Awareness-Raising Questions

1. Name one thing you are aware of in the space around you.
2. Example answer: 'a notepad'.

1. Name one or more *sensory* qualities of that thing you are aware of.
2. Example answer: 'white' and 'made of paper'.

1. Can you distinguish between the thing and the space around it? (Yes)
2. Could you be aware of the thing without a space in which to be aware of it? (No)

1. Is the space in which you are aware of the thing 'white' or 'made of 'paper'? (No)
2. Is the awareness of the thing 'white' or 'made of paper? (No)

1. Name one thing you are aware of *inside* you.
   Example answer: 'depression'.
2. Name one or more sensory quality of that 'depression'.
   Example answer: feeling 'heavy' or 'pulled down' into myself.
3. Name one thing in your life that that 'depression' is *itself* an awareness of?
   Example: a feeling of disappointment or anger in relation to another person.

1. Can you let yourself sense and identify with the spaces in which you are aware of both thoughts and things, instead of with those thoughts and things themselves?
2. Can you distinguish between thoughts you are aware of in your head and the inner head space in which you are aware of them? (Yes)

The 'ABC' of 'ABCT'

'A' for Awareness and Action

The aim of ABCT is to cultivate an on-going Awareness of all the different dimensions of our experience within the moment, and at the same time distinguish that awareness from any specific thing we experience or are aware of – including our overall self-experience. Being distinct from anything we are aware of, awareness is what frees us from passive identification with different elements of our mental, emotional and bodily experience. In this way it also allows us to act in ways that are not simply a reaction to our experience of ourselves, other people and the world.

'B' for Bodyhood and Breathing

The term 'mindfulness' is a poor and misleading substitute for 'awareness'. That is because awareness is not a product of 'the mind' or something purely mental. Awareness itself is neither mental nor bodily. It is awareness <u>of</u> our bodies and minds, our bodies *as well* as our minds. Only through awareness of body and mind – not just mental awareness – can we become more aware of the interaction between the direct wordless, bodily dimensions of our experiencing and their mental reflection in thought and language. That is why the cultivation of sustained awareness is impossible without full body awareness – 'bodyfulness' as well as 'mindfulness'. We breathe air through our mouths and noses into our lungs but it is with and through our entire body surface - and all our body's senses – that we breathe in our awareness of ourselves, other people and the world. Awareness of our breathing is the key to awareness of our body and self as a whole. ABCT is about giving ourselves breathing space – time and space in which to simply be aware. Awareness itself is not a product or property of the body or brain, nor bounded by them. It is awareness itself that 'bodies' – taking on countless bodily shapes and communicating through the language of the body as well as through the word.

'C' for Communication and Cogniscence

We do not need to verbally share all the things of which we are silently 'cogniscent' or aware. For that silent awareness of ourselves and others communicates directly <u>to</u> others whether or not we express it in words. Yet both everyday inter-personal communication and counselling or therapeutic communication ('talking cures') are distorted by the belief that verbal 'sharing' is essential for the awakening and communication of awareness. It is the other way round. Only through the direct cultivation of mental, emotional and bodily awareness can we communicate that awareness to others directly – not just 'in words' but 'through the word' ('dia-logically') and through the language of the body. Verbally 'sharing' things we are 'cogniscent' or aware of – not least in counselling or therapy – easily becomes a substitute for silently deepening the direct awareness of them, and thus communicating, silently or through the word, from this deepened awareness.

'ABCT' in contrast to conventional 'Cognitive Therapy'

Traditional forms of 'C.B.T.' – 'Cognitive-Behavioural Therapy' – are now the most highly-promoted form of non-drugs based psychotherapy. Their common and central claim is that it is a "scientific fact" that "our thoughts cause our feelings and behaviours, not external things, like people, situations and events". (National Association of Cognitive Behavioral Therapists). It is absolutely true that our thoughts *about* things affect our emotional reactions *to* them, and may therefore intensify or reinforce habitual feelings or behaviours towards them. Yet someone whose life has just been affected by such 'things'

148

as losing a job – or a bomb wiping out their entire family – will not easily be convinced of the 'scientific fact' that what they are feeling is 'caused' by their thoughts and not these 'things'. For their 'depression' is not a 'thing in itself' – neither a brain disorder nor a mechanical effect of their thoughts. It is the expression of an *awareness* of undeniable things.

Proponents and practitioners of traditional C.B.T. are certainly right in claiming that people can change the way they feel and act by changing the way they think – in particular so-called 'automatic thoughts' they have in response to situations. The simple fact of the matter however, is that we cannot change a single thought or thing without first being aware of it. A thought itself is just as much a thing we are aware of as any other thing – whether a feeling, event, person or object. Yet this subjective awareness of our thoughts is something quite different from turning them into objects of our mind or intellect – *objects of other thoughts*. The practice of C.B.T. on the other hand, rests on the therapist turning the client's thoughts into clinical objects of the therapist's own 'scientific' thoughts. That is why, although their focus may be on the client's 'automatic thoughts' and their unwanted emotional effects, most 'Cognitive Behavioural Therapists' are unaware of the paradox that their own 'Cognition' of their clients and their Therapeutic Behaviour towards them is shaped by thoughts no less 'automatic' than those of their clients - albeit ones that spring from their supposedly 'scientific' theories. Like traditional CBT, ABCT is essentially a form of 'psycho-education' - specifically 'Education in Awareness'. For in contrast to CBT it recognises that awareness as such – being both thought-free and thing-free - can instantly and automatically free us from identifying emotionally with 'automatic' thoughts about things. And yet we cannot be aware of our thoughts without giving ourselves *Time to Be Aware* – the very essence of both therapy and meditation.

'Awareness Based Cognitive Therapy' could also be termed 'Re-cognitive Behavioural Therapy'. That is because awareness is what allows us to recognise our thoughts about things as just that – thoughts. This prevents us from confusing our thoughts with the very things they are about - for example with the events they might be a response to or the feelings they may seek to give expression to. Recognising thoughts *as* thoughts is what prevents us from both identifying with our thoughts and from identifying thoughts about reality with reality. Yet to recognise thoughts *as* thoughts means being aware of them as 'things in themselves' – albeit 'thought-things' that we experience in our inner mind space, and not the sort of 'things' we experience in physical space. C.B.T. declares it to be an objective "scientific fact" that it is thoughts, not things, that cause people to feel and act the way they do. In contrast, neither Thoughts *nor* Things can in any way 'cause' people to act or feel the way they do if they are aware of *both* as distinct things.

Awareness Based Therapy and the 'Doctrine of Recognition'

The Awareness Principle and **Awareness Based Cognitive Therapy** both have their roots in the 'Doctrine of Recognition' central to the tantric philosophies of 'Kashmir Shaivism', as expounded by its principal teachers or 'gurus' – Somananda, Utpaladeva, Abhinavagupta and Kshemaraja. At the heart of the Doctrine of Recognition is the understanding that ultimate reality has the character of an unbounded space or field of awareness that is the source of all things and that comes to recognise itself in each and every thing experienced within it. Like The Awareness Principle, the 'Doctrine of Recognition' recognises all 'experiencing' and all 'cognition' as essentially subjective – *not* as a 'cognition' of 'objects' by isolated 'subjects' or 'selves', but as the *self-recognition* of universal subjectivity or awareness in every thing it experiences.

"things that have fallen to the level of [being seen as] objects of cognition … are [in reality] essentially awareness"

Utpaladeva

We do not cognise our bodies primarily as 'objects', of perception or reflection. Instead we experience them - subjectively - from within. The same principle applies not only to our experience of our own bodies but to our entire experience of the world around us and every 'thing' within it. For these too, are not essentially 'objects' of perception or reflection but an experiential reflection of a transcendental 'witnessing' awareness or subjectivity. Similarly, what we call 'thinking' does not turn things we experience into 'objects' of 'cognition' or mental 'reflection'. Instead thought itself IS the reflection of direct *subjective* awareness of all we experience. It is through the self-reflection of awareness in both things and thoughts that awareness comes to *recognise* itself in both.

That is why, as long as we continue to even *think* of things as mere 'objects' of 'cognition' – whether sensory, emotional or intellectual – we fail to achieve a state of truly awareness-based or 'recognitive' experiencing. For aware experiencing means being able to *distinguish* each and every thing we experience from the very awareness of experiencing it – the 'Fundamental Distinction' central to ABCT. The *intellectual* understanding and recognition of this distinction in thought is itself central to applying it in life. For in the practice of awareness through ABCT, there is no contradiction whatsoever between use of the thinking intellect and abiding in meditative thought-free awareness. That is because both teachings and *practices* are based on The Awareness Principle – the understanding that the awareness of a thought or concept is *in principle* both thought-free and concept-free. The very terms and concepts of ABCT, as expressed in its Basic Axioms and Maxims, are therefore themselves recognitions of an awareness that is free of verbal concepts – that awareness which, according to the Vijnanabhairava Tantra *"is always a subject and never an object."* As such they can serve as 'mantra' by which to guard ('-tra') that object-free awareness ('man') and to liberate ourselves through it.

MORE ON THE AWARENESS PRINCIPLE

The Traditional Exposition

Awareness is the Self.
Awareness, Shiva, is the soul of the world.
Thus, identifying individual awareness with universal awareness and attaining divine bliss, from where or from whom should one get scared?

For the Yogi who has attained the state of Bhairava [Shiva]
the entire world is experienced as their body.

The Shiva Sutras

Meditate on one's own body as the universe,
and as having the nature of awareness.

The Yogi is always mindful of that witnessing awareness
… which is always a subject and never an object.

The Vijnanabhairava Tantra

Shiva is the Self shining in all things,
All-pervasive, all quiescent Awareness.

May the Shiva in-penetrated into my limited self through his power, offer
worship to the Shiva of the expansive Self
– the concealer of himself by himself!

Somananda

Having made itself manifest, awareness abides
as both the inner and the outer.
The visible world is the body.

Utpaladeva

... the being of all things that are recognised in awareness in turn depends on awareness.

... the power of space is inherent in the soul as true subjectivity, which is at once empty of objects and which also provides a place in which objects may be known.

The Shastras [teachings] and Agamas [scriptures] proclaim with reasoned argument that it [awareness] is free of thought-constructs and precedes all mental representation of any objects.

Just as a man who has been ill for a long time forgets his past pain completely when he regains his health, absorbed as he is in the ease of his present condition, so too are those who are grounded in pure awareness free of thought-constructs no longer conscious of their previous [fettered] state.

The yogi should abide firmly fixed in his own nature by the power of expanding awareness ... relishing the objects of sense that spontaneously appear before him.

'Bhairava' is he whose light shines in the minds of those yogis who are intent on assimilating time into the eternal present of awareness.

Listen! Our Lord [Shiva] whose nature is awareness, is unlimited, the absolute master of the arising and dissolving away of every power.

The power that resides in the Heart of Awareness is Freedom itself.

Abhinavagupta

Every appearance owes its existence to the light of awareness.
Nothing can have its own being without the light of awareness.

Kshemaraja

Awareness as Sole Possible 'Theory of Everything'

In an earlier, wiser age, what today we call 'Theories of Everything' used to be called 'religions' or 'philosophies' and their proponents were pious thinkers or 'philosophers' rather than 'physicists'. Simple philosophical reflection tells us that without prior *awareness* of a universe of things, there can be no theory about *anything* – let alone a theory of 'everything'. It is only because we insist on regarding awareness itself *as* a thing - or as an evolutionary 'property' only of certain types of thing (biological organisms in particular) that we are blinded to the truth of an age-old 'Theory of Everything' – namely that Awareness itself *is* everything. Not awareness *of* some thing or other, nor simply human subjective awareness – 'my' awareness or 'yours' – but Awareness as such, capitalised.

The philosophy that 'Awareness is Everything' and its converse – namely that 'Everything is Awareness' – is what I term 'The Awareness Principle'. This Principle challenges every search for a 'Theory of Everything' grounded purely in physics, and aiming to find it in the form of some super-complex mathematical relation, of matter, energy, space and time. For as the philosopher Martin Heidegger noted, the nature and presuppositions of physics are not themselves the possible object of any possible physical experiment but are something that needs to be thought through meta-physically - philosophically. If we even begin to *think* the nature of physics philosophically we see immediately that, far from being evidentially, experimentally or 'empirically' grounded, it ignores the most self-evident, 'empirical' starting point of scientific inquiry – which is not the *objective existence* of a universe of matter, energy space and time but the *subjective awareness* of it.

I use the term 'Awareness' (capitalised) rather than "our awareness" deliberately – because The Awareness Principle also challenges the presupposition that awareness is necessarily the *private property* of separate bodies or beings. Instead it proposes that all bodies and beings are but individualised shapes, patterns and qualities taken by Awareness as such, that beings only perceive each other *as* 'bodies' in the first place within *fields* of awareness – and do so according to the particular way their individual awareness *fields* are perceptually and conceptually patterned. 'Concepts' themselves are not just ideas in our heads and minds – detached from the universe they seek to represent. Instead they are but the conceptual expression of highly individualised and species-specific field-patterns of awareness – patterns that shape each species' and each individual's entire *perception* of the universe, not least our own scientific *conceptions* of it and theories 'about' it.

This brings us to a new and revolutionary philosophical aspect of The Awareness Principle, namely the understanding it brings that Awareness is not something localised in our heads or in individual organs or organisms, but has an essentially non-local or *field* character. Having the character of an unbounded spatial and temporal field, Awareness is – *in principle* – irreducible to and unexplainable by any thing or things we are aware of as (localised) phenomena *within* this field, any localised objects and any localised 'subjects' of awareness too. Thus to even seek to 'explain' awareness as the product of some localisable thing we are aware *of* (the human brain for example) makes no more sense than to see *dreaming* – the entire *field* of our dreaming awareness – as something reducible to, caused or explicable by some particular, localisable thing that we happen to *dream of* within this field. Even if we happened to repeatedly dream an image of a brain, who would even 'dream' of taking this as evidence that *dreaming as such* is a property of this particular *dreamt object*? Yet this is *the* essential error of materialistic body- and brain-based accounts of 'mind', 'consciousness' and awareness, forgetting as they do that the brain itself is but one localisable phenomenon within the larger field of human *waking*

158

awareness – and that this field too is *in principle* irreducible to any one Thing that appears within it.

The principle that awareness has a field character, and therefore cannot in principle be reduced to or explained by anything we are aware of within that field, is one of the basic axioms or 'first principles' of 'The Awareness Principle'. Its most essential 'first principle' is that Awareness as such – and not any thing we perceive or conceive of within it, is itself necessarily the 'First Principle' of the universe – being the precondition for our awareness *of* anything and everything, and thus the precondition too for any possible 'Theory of Everything'. Understanding this, the only *possible* 'Theory of Everything' is The Awareness Principle itself – the understanding that Awareness is Everything and Everything is Awareness. For just as there can *in principle* be nothing 'outside' space, so can there be nothing outside Awareness - no 'Thing' to study or invent 'Theories' about. The Awareness Principle simply recognises Awareness as that which is in principle the sole or absolute reality – leading to a theory, which must necessarily understand all things as manifestations or materialisations of Awareness.

The Awareness Principle achieves this understanding only by undermining a principal unquestioned presupposition of both scientists and academic philosophers - namely that Awareness is necessarily the property of separate, localised beings or bodies. Yet as long as *religionists* too, cling onto the belief that 'God' is some sort of being 'with' awareness, rather than being identical *with* Awareness (an age-old Indian religious philosophy) they fall into the same trap as – and therefore fall prey to – the atheistic arguments of scientists such as Richard Dawkins or philosophers such as Daniel Dennett. For it is only because they *also* cling to the misconception that Awareness is necessarily the private property of beings in the form of biological organisms or organs – the brain in particular – that they so firmly believe 'God' to be a mere figment of *human* beings and of the evolutionary biology of their brains.

All current scientific 'Theories of Everything' are essentially the same Theory – the Theory that the universe consists solely of 'Things'. Within the terms of this unstated 'Theory of Everything', and in contrast to The Awareness Principle, 'Things' themselves are necessarily seen as preconditions for sentience, consciousness or awareness, thus awareness is necessarily seen as a product or by-product of some Thing, and effectively reduced to a 'Thing' in itself. It is in the light of such a grand, dogmatic, unstated and above all unquestioned 'Theory of Everything' that we can truly heed the words of Martin Heidegger: "Science IS the new religion." For all would-be physical-scientific 'Theories of Everything' amount to nothing more than a *religiously* held *belief* that the universe consists of nothing more than 'Things' – thus totally forgetting that Awareness of Things is prior *in principle* to any possible Theory of them, and that therefore Awareness as such cannot *in principle* be reduced to or explained by any 'Thing' whatsoever. Such "in principle" recognitions express the essence of 'The Awareness Principle', together with the consequent affirmation that The Awareness Principle *itself* is the sole basis for a 'Theory' of that which ultimately lies behind 'Everything' – for it is the only Theory that recognises that any and every 'Thing' is essentially a phenomenon 'emerging' from and within fields of awareness, and ultimately from within that unbounded and infinite field of awareness which *alone* deserves to be recognised and religiously revered as 'God' – and must be if God is not to be reduced to one being among others we are aware *of*. Awareness as such is not only the source of what we call matter and energy, but is also the essence of what we call 'soul' and 'spirit', indeed the essence of *God* as such. All this is anathema to that science, now elevated to the status of a religion, that has forgotten the very meaning of its name – 'physics'.

The term 'physics' derives from the Greek *physis* and means to 'emerge', just as the term 'phenomenon' comes from the Greek *phainesthai* – meaning 'to show itself', and the word 'existence' has the root meaning of 'to stand out' or 'ex-ist'. The Awareness Principle whilst indeed a *philosophical* 'Theory of Everything', is also one that at the same time understands all Things as *physical phenomena* in the truest, most radical or 'root' sense of these words – as things that can in principle only be seen to 'emerge from', 'show themselves' and 'stand out' ('ex-ist') within Awareness as such - understood as the very context or *field* from and within which they do so. 'A' for Awareness is truly the missing factor in Einstein's famous equation: $e = mc^2$. For not even such a thing as 'light', whose speed is a basic and invariable factor in this equation, would be visible were it not for the invisible *light of awareness* in which alone all things, including 'physical' light itself, can emerge, show themselves and ex-ist or stand out. To explain such phenomena as light itself in purely mathematical terms as abstract 'quanta' is not to bring science closer to the underlying reality of the universe, but infinitely further away from what is immediately evident to each and all of us - namely that we could not be aware of anything, let alone develop a 'Theory of Everything' without the simple experiential fact of us being first of all *aware* of a universe of things. And just as no objects are perceptible or even *conceivable* without a space surrounding them, nor is our awareness of anything in space conceivable without a *spacious field of awareness*. The recognition that space and time themselves are not essentially 'objective' or 'physical' dimensions of the universe but innate dimensions of *subjective awareness* was bequeathed to Western Philosophy centuries ago by Immanuel Kant – and much, much earlier – by Indian religious philosophers. When will our modern physicists, with their would-be 'Theories of Everything' begin to heed this heritage, instead of priding themselves on the 'objectivity' of their Theories and denying the essentially *subjective* nature of all experiencing and of 'Everything' we experience?

In this respect, not only today's scientists with their crude conceptions of the universe, but also their current religionist enemies, with their crude and unquestioned concepts of God, would both do well to be reminded of such already clear affirmations of 'The Awareness Principle' as I cite below. These affirmations stem neither from priests, physicists or purely academic 'philosophers of mind' but from the most pious thinkers of 10th century India, giving expression to truths recognised by other sages centuries before them:

**"… the being of all things that are recognised
in awareness in turn depends on awareness."**

**"… space is inherent in the soul as true subjectivity
which is at once empty of objects and which also
provides a place in which objects may be known."**

Abhinavagupta

**"Every appearance owes its existence to the light of awareness.
Nothing can have its own being without the light of awareness."**

Kshemaraja

Awareness as the First Principle of Science

From any experiential or 'empirical' point of view, the most fundamental scientific 'fact' is not what science takes it to be – the objective existence of a universe of 'things' in space-time. On the contrary, the most self-evidential, empirical and therefore scientific fact is our subjective awareness of ourselves, and of a universe of things. That very awareness of things however, is not itself a thing – nor can it be explained by or reduced to any thing or things we are aware of. To even attempt to do so would be like attempting to explain or reduce our dreaming awareness to some particular thing we dream of.

The 'First Principle' of 'The Awareness Principle' is that Awareness itself – and not any thing or universe of things we are aware of - is the First Principle of the universe.

Every aspect and application of The Awareness Principle comes from the recognition that awareness comes first – not matter, energy or any 'thing' or world of 'things'. The underlying but unquestioned, untestable, unprovable and fundamentally *counter-intuitive* principle of current science is that awareness can somehow emerge from a basically insentient or *unaware* universe of space and time, matter and energy. How awareness could arise from this unaware universe is not just something temporarily inexplicable, and therefore a subject of scientific hypothesis. It is inexplicable *in principle*. For just as the starting point of all inquiries into the nature of the universe is awareness of that universe, so is the starting point of all scientific inquiries into awareness nothing but awareness itself. Every 'scientific' attempt to explain the origins or basis of 'consciousness' or 'awareness' through something outside or beyond awareness is scientifically impossible in principle – the very attempt and all the experiments that go along with it being something that occur within the awareness of the scientist.

The primary purpose of The Awareness Principle, as a new foundation for life and science, is to rescue life itself from domination by the unquestioned, non-scientific presuppositions of what is, in reality a purely Western concept of 'science'. That does not mean returning to the dead ends of paganism or religious fundamentalism, Eastern or Western, Oriental or Occidental, Southern or Nordic. Neither does it mean retreating into the realm of personal lived experience, secular or spiritual (for in today's world even this realm is insidiously shaped by popularised Western-scientific concepts, concepts which shape the world in which each individual lives through their ruthless application in fields as diverse as government and economics, medicine and psychiatry, and even counselling and psychotherapy). Instead, the aim of The Awareness Principle – to rescue both personal and social life from domination by the abstract presuppositions of science – is one that can only be achieved by rescuing the whole Western concept of science from these unquestioned presuppositions. Principal among these root presuppositions is the identification of truth with 'objects' and 'objectivity'. The Awareness Principle challenges this whole 'Objectivity Principle' of Western Science – instead reasserting the primary truth and absolute reality of 'subjectivity'. Precursors of The Awareness Principle can be found in Indian philosophy, in European 'phenomenology', in Gestalt psychology and psychoanalysis. None of these precursors of The Awareness Principle however – besides those found in Indian Advaitic and Tantric philosophy – explicitly articulated its First Principle. Nor did they properly conceptualise its 'Second Principle'.

The Second Principle of The Awareness Principle is that Awareness as such is inseparable but also quite distinct from each and every thing we are aware of.

Out of this principle comes what I call The Fundamental Choice – a choice that each of us can make at any moment of our lives. The choice is whether to identify with things we are aware of or 'experience' – whether in the form of desires and impulses, sensations or perceptions, emotions or events – or, on the other hand, to identify with the very awareness of them; recognising that awareness as something essentially distinct from each and every thing we 'experience' or are aware of within it, including ourselves.

The Third Principle of Awareness is that it embraces, pervades and transcends all that we can experience or be aware of.

The relation between awareness as such and all that we are aware of can be compared to the relation between space and the things we perceive in it. Space embraces each object within it, yet whilst it is inseparable from each of the objects within it, it is not itself an object – and transcends all the objects within it. Objects have location – we can say where they are 'in' space. Space itself on the other hand has an essentially non-local or 'field' character – we cannot say 'where' space is. Similarly, whereas we can localise each and every object or thing we are aware of – for example localising an object in space, a sensation in our bodies or a thought in our heads – we cannot localise the awareness of it – we cannot say where our awareness of anything is. The most important of Indian treatises on awareness placed great importance on the yogic practice of identifying with the space around and within things. That is because they understood and experienced the reality that space, like time, is not essentially an objective dimension of the universe at all but a basic dimension of subjectivity - of awareness.

The Fourth Principle of the Awareness Principle is that everything we are aware of *is itself* an awareness, and a doorway to an entire awareness world.

A sound we hear is not just something we are aware of, but it is an awareness of something else – a passing car, a conversation, a bird singing. Yet the bird too is not just something we are aware of but is itself an awareness of a unique sort. Its song is an expression of that awareness. The bird's awareness is very different from ours, and it is that which is echoed in the sound of its song – in the same way that any singer's awareness is. Similarly, when we hear a car horn honking in a busy street, this is not just a sound we are aware of. Indeed we only hear the sound *as* 'a car honking' because the sound we are aware of is an awareness - of a car honking. That awareness of a car horn honking is in turn an awareness too of the stress or anger of the driver honking the horn, of the driver's awareness of the traffic, and/or their awareness of feeling stressed or impatient.

Simply reading a text or hearing a person speak we are not just aware of words. Indeed we are only aware of words *as* words because we are aware of them as expressions of another awareness – the awareness of the speaker or writer. In general, any thought, mood, emotion, perception, action or bodily sensation is not just something we are aware of but *is* an awareness of some aspect of ourselves or others, of our world, our relationships or life situation. What we label as 'stress', 'tension', 'anxiety' and 'depression' are not things in themselves that we happen to feel. They are a felt awareness of important aspects of our lives, life relationships and life world. And there is nothing we can ever be aware of in the world that is *not itself* an awareness. Just as fright is an awareness of something in the surrounding world, even a stone is aware of its environment, indeed *is* an awareness of its own environmental world. Every 'thing' we are aware of in the world is aware of a world of things as a whole, experiencing its own unique *awareness world* – whether that of a stone, bird or another human being. The higher level awareness that everything we are aware of is an awareness of something else within our awareness world, and that this 'something else' is also an awareness – indeed an entire awareness world in itself – *this* awareness is what expands our awareness to embrace new awareness worlds. The Awareness Principle recognises that we are part of an ever-

166

expanding multi-dimensional universe of awareness embracing countless things - each an awareness in itself and each part of its own unique awareness world. The expanding nature of the physical universe is an expression of the innately expansive character of awareness itself, which constantly opens up new worlds of awareness from within itself.

The 1st Principle of the Awareness Principle

1. The central axiom or 'First Principle' of 'The Awareness Principle' is that Awareness itself – and not any thing or universe of things we are aware of – IS the First Principle of the universe.

2. Awareness is the 'transcendental' condition – the 'pre-condition' or 'field condition' – for our awareness of any thing or universe of things whatsoever.

3. Awareness embraces and transcends all that we experience or are aware of – all 'contents' of consciousness and all elements of our experience.

4. Just as dreaming cannot be explained by or reduced to anything we dream of, nor can awareness be explained by or reduced to any thing or things we are aware of (for example matter or energy, the body or brain chemistry).

5. Just as space is inseparable but at the same time quite distinct from every object in it, so is awareness inseparable and at the same time quite distinct from each and every thing we are aware of.

6. Just as space embraces, permeates and transcends every object in it, so does awareness embrace, permeate and transcend everything we are aware of.

7. Awareness of things is not itself a thing. Thus awareness of a localised object in space is not itself a localised object in space – it is non-local and object-free.

8. Awareness of a bodily sensation or symptom, drive or impulse, action or behavioural pattern, emotion or thought is not itself a sensation or symptom, drive or impulse, action or behavioural pattern, and is therefore intrinsically free of all such contents of consciousness.

9. Everything we are aware of also is an awareness. A feeling is an awareness of something – and not just something we are aware of, and so is a bodily sensation or symptom. Awareness is therefore not only 'transcendent' but also 'immanent' - present within all things.

Axioms of the Awareness Principle (1)

1. We assume that without a world of things there would be no aware beings and nothing to be aware of. It is the other way round. Without awareness there would be nothing, no thing and no world, to be aware of and no aware beings.

2. Awareness cannot – in principle – be a property or by-product of any body or being, thing or object, self or 'subject', ego or 'I' that we are aware of.

3. Awareness as such, and any thing we are aware of, are like space and objects in space. They are both inseparable and yet absolutely distinct.

4. Everything we are aware of has a localisable character – it can be localised in space. Awareness, like space, has an essentially non-local or 'field' character.

5. Space has an inside but there can be nothing 'outside' space. Similarly there can be nothing outside awareness.

6. Since there is nothing outside awareness, everything we are aware of exists within awareness, and can be nothing but a form taken by awareness.

7. 'Energy' (Greek *energein*) is not a thing but the formative activity of awareness through which it actualises or gives shape to itself in everything we are aware of.

8. Consciousness is awareness OF things, rather than awareness as such. Since without awareness there would be nothing to be aware of, awareness is the pre-condition for all 'conscious' experiencing.

9. Awareness has its own innate field-patterns and sensual qualities, actual and potential, these being the inner source of all the patterns and sensory qualities that make up the physical universe as we know it.

10. Any physically manifest or actual pattern or quality of awareness is automatically stabilised through self-resonance with its reality as a potential pattern or quality of awareness as such.

11. All sensory qualities that we are aware OF – colour, shape, texture etc. - are expressions of innate sensual qualities, shapes and textures OF awareness as such.

12. All shapes, patterns and qualities of awareness are essentially TONAL shapes, patterns and qualities – like the qualities of warmth and coldness, hardness and softness, brightness or darkness etc. that belong to musical or vocal tones, and their patterning as sounds.

13. The primary property of awareness however, is its 'I'-ness or 'Self-hood' – its 'self-recognition' in and through its manifestation in every entity or 'being' we can be aware of - whether thing or person, object or subject.

14. Awareness of Being is the primary property of awareness as such. Awareness cannot in principle be the private property of any particular ego, self or 'I' – for Being, Self-hood or 'I'-ness is ITS primary property.

15. Since Awareness of Being is the very Being of Awareness, Awareness is 'ontologically' and 'epistemologically' prior to both 'Being' and 'beings' – the absolute and primordial reality that lies behind all things.

Axioms of the Awareness Principle (2)

1. **Awareness** is not a by-product of matter or energy. Instead, just as matter is the perceived *outwardness* of 'energy' i.e. of *action* as it manifests in the world, so is the *inwardness* the realm of potentiality from which all action and actualities spring.

2. **Awareness** is not a product of the body or brain. How can it be, since bodies and brains have reality only *in* our awareness?

3. **Awareness** is not bounded by our physical bodies. How can it be, since our awareness of the space around our bodies is nothing itself but a spatial field *of* awareness?

4. **Awareness** is not the property of a localised 'subject', 'self', 'ego' or 'I' – How can it be, since all localised 'subjects' of awareness only know themselves as centres of a *non-local* space or 'field' of awareness?

5. **Awareness** is not a blank sheet on which we receive impressions of an external sensory world. How can it be, since awareness has its own *innate sensual qualities* – such as the sensed light and darkness, levity and gravity, colour and tone of our moods, or the sensed density or diffuseness, clarity or dullness of our everyday consciousness?

6. **Awareness** is immaterial, but it is nothing shapeless, disembodied or insubstantial. How can it be, since our own body is nothing but the sensed bodily shape and substantiality *of* our awareness?

7. **Awareness** is not a product of energetic patterns or material forms, of genetic or molecular patterns or biological forms. How can it be, since pattern and form are themselves nothing material or energetic? You can no more pick up or hold the *pattern* of a molecule, cell or biological form than you can pick up or hold the pattern of a geometric form, the roundness of a circle or the squareness of a square.

8. **Awareness** is not a pattern or form, but it forms or crystallises itself into patterns, just as it also flows in draughts and currents like air and water, mixes and merges in streams, radiates and ripples in and out like waves of energy, diffuses and densifies like matter.

9. **Awareness** does not require any energetic, material or 'aetheric' medium in which to take form or flow, radiate or ripple in waves, move or communicate. Awareness *is* the aether.

10. **Awareness** does not require physical time or space or motion as its medium. How can it, since our very awareness of physical motion in space and time is preceded by motions of awareness, occurring in times and spaces of our awareness? The Olympic diver preparing to dive does not first move his body and *then* become aware of this physical movement. On the contrary, the precise physical movement of his body in space and time is the expression of a precisely rehearsed inner motion of his bodily awareness as such.

11. **Awareness** is not simply awareness *of* some *localised* object or 'thing' that is already *present* - 'out there' or 'in ourselves' – thus enabling us to focus on it and reflect on it in thought. How can it be, since all things and all thoughts – all phenomena whatsoever that we experience – only *come to presence* within *non-local* spaces or *fields* of awareness?

12. **Awareness** is not bound by our experience *of* phenomena – whether things or thoughts, percepts or concepts, sensations or emotions, drives or impulses. How can it be, since just as our awareness of an experienced object *is not* that object, neither is our *awareness* of experiencing any phenomenon the same thing as that experienced phenomenon?

13. **Awareness** is not a relation of a localised subject to a localised object. How can it be, since all localised subjects or objects of awareness only arise within non-local fields of awareness? Objects are the outward form taken by innate field-patterns and field-qualities of awareness or subjectivity. Awareness is itself a subjective field and field-pattern of awareness. 'Objects' are but a medium of intersubjectivity - the perception of one 'consciousness' or 'subjectivity' - one *field-pattern of awareness* - within the perceptual environment or *patterned field of awareness* of another.

Axioms of the Awareness Principle (3)

1. The *awareness* of an experience – be it a colour or sound, a thought or perception, impulse or emotion, word or action, pain or pleasure, *is not* that experience.

2. Bondage and ignorance both come about through *identification* with elements of one's experience – whether one's experienced self or its experienced world.

3. Our experienced self and world is constantly changing, unless it is bound and rigidified by identification with specific elements of our experience.

4. Every experience 'we' have is, paradoxically, an experience of something other-than-self (whether an object or another person).

5. Every experience of something other-than-self, is something that can affect and lend a different quality to our self-experience – our way of experiencing ourselves.

6. The three basic dimensions of experience are: our self-experience, our experience of the world and other people, and the activity of experiencing. At the heart of this threefold (*trika*) – and distinct from it – is *awareness*.

7. The activity of experiencing is a dynamic *interactivity* between our experience of self and our experience of otherness.

8. If we regard all experiencing as an activity of the self alone, and treat all our experiences as the private property of that self, we block the process of experiencing.

9. Only through *awareness* of the process of experiencing can we allow *what* we experience to affect our sense of *who* we are - letting our experience of other people and the world transform our *self-experience*.

10. True 'self-awareness' is awareness of our bodily self-experience at any given time, allowing it to be affected and transformed by our experience of *others and otherness*.

11. Awareness frees our felt experience of both self and world, allowing it to transform from minute to minute, hour to hour, day to day, week to week, month to month, year to year, decade to decade, lifetime to lifetime.

12. Allowing our experienced self and experienced world to change means that personal identity is no longer dependent on identification with past memories - since neither the remembering 'self' nor its remembered world remain fixed.

13. We are only truly *aware* of our *experienced self and world* as a whole to the extent that we are aware of our *experienced body as a whole*.

14. Only through attention to our direct *bodily experience* of ourselves, other people and the world, can we attain awareness of our *experienced body* as a whole.

15. Only awareness of our experienced body as a whole - *total body awareness* - releases us from identification with a particular experience of self and world.

16. Only this total awareness of our bodily self-experience makes us sensitive to the self-experience of other beings – *their* bodily experience of self and world.

17. Awareness has its own intrinsic sensual qualities – of spatiality and substantiality, light and darkness, warmth and coolness, levity and gravity, tone and texture.

18. Only through attention to the innate sensual qualities of awareness can we begin to sense our own souls and those of others.

19. Our entire *sensory* experience of ourselves, other people and the world, and every *sensory* quality of our experience, is an expression of specific *sensual* qualities of awareness or 'soul qualities'.

20. Our soul-body is nothing but a more or less permeable field-boundary of awareness – one that can either separate our *self-experience* from our experience of the world and other people - or allow them to affect, transform and enrich one another.

21. Bondage is the rigidification of our soul-body as an *awareness boundary*, transforming it into an *identity boundary* that artificially separates our self-experience from all that we experience as 'other than self'.

22. Bondage is also the reduction of our self-experience to a set of limited and limiting identifications with a fixed set of soul qualities.

23. Awareness frees us from limited and limiting identifications, at the same time allowing us to freely identify with *others* and with *other* elements of our experience.

24. Awareness has no fixed 'self' or 'subject'. All that we experience both as 'self' and as 'other-than-self' is one *self-expression* of an unbounded field of free awareness.

25. The transcendental *free-awareness field* that is *Shiva* is what unites the individual soul or awareness field (*Jiva*) with the souls of all others and with the world soul.

26. It does so through its multiplicity of infinitesimal centres of awareness and through its infinite multiplicity of immanent soul-qualities or *Shaktis*.

27. This very unity of *Jiva* with *Shiva* and his *Shaktis* is the supreme triad or *Paratrika* – a triad whose heart is an awareness with no fixed centre and no finite circumference.

28. Awareness is what allows us to freely *form and transform* our experiential reality from an infinite multiplicity of soul qualities. Awareness is therefore freedom (*moksha*) and liberation in this very life (*jivanmukti*) through *Shiva-Shakti*.

29. The Absolute Awareness or Subjectivity that is *Shiva* is neither a person or being, nor an impersonal force or energy. It is the supreme unbounded awareness field that is the source of all beings and all persons. We, no less than the gods themselves, are multiple and ever-changing *personifications* of this divine field, and of its divine soul qualities or *Shaktis*.

The Philosophy of Absolute Subjectivism

The Awareness Principle, understood as a philosophical position, can be termed 'Absolute Subjectivism'. That is because its major axiom or first principle is that awareness or subjectivity is itself the 'first principle' and source of all that is - and not any possible 'object' of consciousness. In essence there simply are no such things as 'objects' - for there can be nothing 'outside' awareness or subjectivity. Our lived experience of things and the entire world of things that constitutes that lived experience is intrinsically subjective. All experience, whether reflective or pre-reflective, whether of thoughts or things, inner or 'outer' worlds, is essentially subjective. Absolute Subjectivism is the recognition that subjectivity as such – which I term 'awareness' - is the sole possible absolute, being the transcendental or 'a priori' condition for our experience not only of any possible 'object' but also of any possible ego or 'I', subject or self, world or universe. Awareness, understood as 'absolute' or 'transcendental' subjectivity, is neither the product of any object, nor the property of any subject ('empirical' or 'transcendental'). Just as there is nothing 'outside' space, so there is nothing outside awareness. Just as space transcends every thing that stands out or 'ex-ists' within it, so does absolute subjectivity - 'awareness' - transcend every thing we experience within it. Absolute Subjectivism abolishes the presupposition of Transcendental Phenomenology that subjectivity is necessarily the property of an ego or 'I', subject or self, being or body and the 'scientific' myth that subjectivity or awareness can - even in principle - be understood as the product of any 'thing' we can experience within it – such as the human brain. Like space, there is nothing outside awareness. Yet it possesses an infinite interiority that embraces not only all actual things but all potential realities - the unbounded potentialities of awareness immanent within every thing. Awareness is thus not only transcendent but also immanent within every thing and every being. Even seemingly insentient or inorganic 'things' such as atoms, molecules, clouds and rocks are in reality aware or sentient beings. The fact that human beings no longer experience their subjective awareness or 'spirit' is the sole reason why we now perceive them only as 'objects'. In reality all beings are all distinct 'subjectivities' or 'consciousnesses', not separate or apart from one another but each a distinct and inseparable part of an absolute subjectivity or divine awareness. Individual subjectivities or consciousnesses are individualisations of this absolute subjectivity. Ordinary thought and sense-perception objectify other subjectivities or consciousnesses. It is this activity of objectification – itself a process occurring within awareness – that gives beings the apparent character of subjects separate from one another and from a world of 'objects'.

Awareness as Absolute Subjectivity

1. Awareness, as Subjectivity independent of any specific self or subject, ego or 'I', body or being, is Absolute – the ultimate reality and source of all that is.

2. Awareness, as Absolute Subjectivity, is the pre-condition or 'transcendental' condition for our experience of any self or subject, thing or object, body or being.

3. Awareness, as Absolute Subjectivity cannot therefore, in principle, be the product of any being or body, thing or object we are aware of.

4. Awareness, as Absolute Subjectivity, cannot also, in principle, be the property of any ego or 'I', self or 'subject' we are aware of.

5. Awareness, as Absolute Subjectivity knows no 'objects', internal or external, but permeates all experiencing, inner and outer. All experiencing is in principle subjective - not the cognition of an object by a subject.

6. Awareness, as Absolute Subjectivity is distinct, in principle, from any self, thing or world we experience, anything that we are or can be aware of.

7. Awareness, as Absolute Subjectivity, has, in principle, no external boundaries or 'outside'. Just as there can, in principle, be nothing 'outside' space, so there can, in principle, be nothing 'outside' awareness.

8. Awareness, as Absolute Subjectivity, is, in principle, like space and time, being both distinct and inseparable from all we experience or are aware of within them.

9. Awareness, as Absolute Subjectivity, unlike space, has an unbounded interiority or 'inside' - including not only all actual but all potential experiences and experiential worlds.

10. Awareness, as Absolute Subjectivity, takes the form of bounded units or 'bodies' of awareness, each with their own individualised shapes and patterns of awareness. A 'subjectivity' or 'consciousness' – whether in the form of a 'thing', 'being' or 'self' - is such a bounded unit or body of awareness.

11. Awareness, as Absolute Subjectivity has a non-local or field character. The entire universe and all universes are its body. Every individualised 'consciousness' or subjectivity, by contrast, is a bounded and localised unit or body of awareness.

12. Awareness, as Absolute Subjectivity, does not only take the form of 'living organisms'. Not just every atom and molecule but every cell and organ of our body is an aware or 'sentient' organism in itself - distinct but inseparable from the organism as a whole, defined by its organising field-patterns of awareness.

13. Awareness, as Absolute Subjectivity, takes the form of field-patterns and patterned fields of awareness. Every individual and species of being is a specific field-pattern of awareness, one which in turn creates its own patterned field of awareness or perceptual 'environment' – whether that of a water drop, rock, plant or animal species, human being or 'higher' consciousness.

Absolute Subjectivism vs the Presuppostions of Science

ACCEPTED PRESUPPOSITION

Reality, truth and true scientific knowledge is objective.

THE AWARENESS PRINCIPLE

Reality, truth, and true scientific knowledge is subjective.

ACCEPTED PRESUPPOSITION

The starting point of science and the most basic scientific 'fact' is the objective existence of a universe of bodies in space-time.

THE AWARENESS PRINCIPLE

The most basic scientific fact is our subjective awareness of a universe of bodies in space and time.

ACCEPTED PRESUPPOSITION

Space and time are objective dimensions of reality in which things 'exist'.

THE AWARENESS PRINCIPLE

Space and time are subjective dimensions of awareness.

ACCEPTED PRESUPPOSITION

The universe is composed of units of matter and energy.

THE AWARENESS PRINCIPLE

The universe is composed of awareness. Energy is the materialisation of awareness.

ACCEPTED PRESUPPOSITION

Awareness or 'subjectivity' is something 'owned' - the private property of an ego or 'I', being or person, self or 'subject'.

THE AWARENESS PRINCIPLE

Awareness is not something we 'own', not the private property of beings, persons, selves or subjects. Instead it is the very source of all individualised beings and all localised subjects.

ACCEPTED PRESUPPOSITION

Awareness is an emergent property or evolutionary by-product of an unaware matter and energy and a property or 'function' of the body.

THE AWARENESS PRINCIPLE

Not just the human body but all bodies are outward shapes taken by awareness in the course of its evolution.

ACCEPTED PRESUPPOSITION

Awareness is something possessed and bounded by bodies in space, like a 'soul' contained within the 'body' and bounded by it.

THE AWARENESS PRINCIPLE

Awareness of the world around us - of the space surrounding our bodies and of other bodies – is not itself bounded by our own body. The soul or psyche is not merely an inner awareness of ourselves but embraces our entire awareness of the world around us.

ACCEPTED PRESUPPOSITION

We are our minds and bodies, thoughts and emotions, impulses and actions, and the way we experience ourselves through them.

THE AWARENESS PRINCIPLE

Our minds and bodies, thoughts and emotions and sensory experience together form our experienced self. We are not our experience or our experienced self. We are the awareness which experiences that self.

ACCEPTED PRESUPPOSITION

Awareness is something localised in the brain and always focussed on some object or 'thing'.

THE AWARENESS PRINCIPLE

Awareness is essentially non-local – a space or field within which we come to experience things and can choose to focus on them.

ACCEPTED PRESUPPOSITION

The mind is a mirror of the world.

THE AWARENESS PRINCIPLE

The mind is a mirror of our awareness of the world.

ACCEPTED PRESUPPOSITION

Subjective awareness is a mirror of the objective, material world.

THE AWARENESS PRINCIPLE

The world is a mirror and a manifestation of subjective awareness.

ACCEPTED PRESUPPOSITION

Awareness is always awareness of something.

THE AWARENESS PRINCIPLE

Awareness is prior to, distinct from and transcends all things we are aware of.

ACCEPTED PRESUPPOSITION

Awareness is the same as 'consciousness' of things.

THE AWARENESS PRINCIPLE

Awareness transcends everything we are aware or 'conscious' of.
The so-called 'unconscious' is not non-awareness but pure awareness.

ACCEPTED PRESUPPOSITION

Things – bodies and beings - are composed of matter and energy.

THE AWARENESS PRINCIPLE

Every 'thing' – every 'body' and 'being' - is an awareness or subjectivity in its own right - a bodily shape and form taken by the divine awareness, which is not only transcendent of but immanent within all things, all bodies and all beings.

From Thinking Being to Thinking Awareness

The Awareness Principle is the principle of that "Other Thinking" anticipated by Martin Heidegger – one that both arises from awareness and one that also thinks the nature of awareness, rather than the nature of 'Being' and of beings. The thinking of Being and beings has been central to the development of Western thought since the inception of philosophy in Greece. It is this mode of thinking that has culminated in the 'Europeanisation of the world' through the global dominance of a purely calculative thinking and science in which subjectivity or awareness is seen only as the private property of the ego, and scientific truth is identified with objectivity rather than subjectivity. In contrast The Awareness Principle heralds the return to Indian metaphysical principles and yogic practices which recognised Awareness rather than Being as the absolute. The Awareness Principle articulates in a new way the implicit or unthought precepts of this tradition, making them clearer and more explicit through recognition of nine basic truths:

1. Awareness ('Chit') has an essentially unbounded, non-local or 'field' character.

2. The absolute awareness field is both the singular and divine source of all beings (the truth of 'monism') but is not itself a single divine being (the myth of 'monotheism').

3. The divine awareness field, as the 'oceanic' source of all beings, can no more be conceived of as one single and 'supreme' being than can the ocean be conceived of as one single and supreme fish.

4. Awareness, as the source of all bodily and sensory experiencing, has itself an innately sensual character and is the source of an infinite multiplicity of sensual qualities and bodily forms.

5. Being the pre-condition for our experience of any being or body, subject or self, object or thing, awareness cannot itself be reduced to the property or product of any being or body, subject or self, object or thing.

6. Awareness ('Shiva') embraces not only being as Actuality, but the reality of non-being - understood as a realm of pure Potentiality – the power or capacity for actualisation ('Shakti').

7. Potential realities, by their very nature, have reality only in awareness, and do so only as those potential shapes, patterns, tones and qualities of awareness that actualise themselves as 'beings' and 'things', subjects and objects.

8. Individualised 'selves', 'souls', 'consciousnesses' or 'beings' are localised field-boundaries of awareness ('bodies') emerging from and within the unbounded and non-local awareness field that is the divine.

9. 'Bodies' are therefore nothing essentially biological, material or energetic – they are the very field-boundaries or boundary-fields of awareness uniting the otherwise unbounded fields or 'spaces' of awareness within and around them.

The Awareness Principle and the 'Spiritual'

The Principles and Practices of Awareness - both in their traditional exposition as millennia-old yogic philosophical principles and practices and in their exposition as 'The New Yoga of Awareness' - share in common a crucial understanding of the 'spiritual', albeit one which is concealed by the very terms 'spirit', 'holy spirit', 'spirituality', 'the spiritual world' etc. Western 'spirituality' gives metaphysical and religious primacy to the notion of 'spirit' as such - even though its nature is never exactly defined. In contrast, Indian religious metaphysics gives primacy to the notion of space or Akasha (pronounced 'aakash'). The Awareness Principle too, understands space as a primary dimension of subjectivity or awareness, indeed as identical with that pure or transcendental awareness which is 'God'. That is why one of the most important if not primary Practices of Awareness advocated in the Shaivist Tantras (in particular the Vijnanabhairavatantra) is the expansion of awareness through identification with space.

The term 'Akasha' is translated both as 'space' and as 'aether' or 'ether'. That is because it is understood as pervaded by awareness in the form of Prana - the primordial 'air', 'wind' or 'breath' of awareness. This is also the root meaning of 'spirit' in its derivation from Latin 'spirare' (to breathe), the term 'spiritus' being a Latin translation of the Greek 'pneuma' (air/wind) and cognate also with the root meaning of the Greek 'psyche' (breath). To be 'spiritual' in the Indian yogic sense is to be capable, quite literally, of a different, more primordial type of re-spiration or breathing. This primordial respiration is a 'transpiration' in which we sense ourselves breathing in our awareness of the clear, luminous expansiveness of the space around us, not through our lungs alone but through every pore of our skin. In this way we can come to experience breathing as an in-breath of the pure 'air' of awareness itself. It is not just the immaterial nature of this higher air or 'aether' of awareness, but this long-lost experience of breathing this immaterial air that lies concealed behind the otherwise vague Western notion of 'spirit'. In contrast it is given much richer definition through the yogic term 'Prana' - understood as that invisible breath or 'air' of awareness that pervades the entirety of space – both the space around us and the space which constitutes the larger part of every atom of 'matter'.

The twin-meaning of 'Akasha' as (1) 'space' and (2) aether, together with the meaning of 'aether' itself as a 'purer', 'higher' – indeed less air-filled and thus more spacious 'air' - is symbolised by the Himalayan mountaintop, both as a place of meditation and as the very abode of Shiva – that deity who is both Lord of Yoga and who personifies and embodies the absolute or divine awareness as such.

Awareness and 'Energy'

The Principle that 'everything is awareness' stands in direct contrast to the dogma - shared by modern science and 'New Age' pseudo-science alike - that everything is 'energy'. As a 'Theory of Everything' this 'Energy Principle' is dogmatic because it rests on a notion of 'energy' that is wholly unquestioned and a gross distortion of its root meaning. Even in modern translations of Tantric metaphysics this Greek derived word is distortedly used to translate the Sanskrit term for the feminine aspect of divinity - 'Shakti'. A far better translation of this word is not 'energy' in its current sense - but 'power', power in the sense of 'power of action' or 'power of actualisation'. This translation of 'Shakti' fully accords with the root meaning of the term 'energy' itself – not as some 'thing' but as the very action or activity (the Greek verb *energein*) that gives form to all things from within that infinite space or 'aether' of awareness known in Sanskrit as 'Akasha'. Today many scientists advance the highly plausible but still unorthodox hypothesis that space is no mere void or vacuum, but an infinite source of 'potential energy' or 'power of action'. This hypothesis is in perfect correspondence with the Tantric understanding of the universe as an expression of countless Shaktis or 'powers of action' emerging within an infinite space or 'aether' of awareness (Akasha) and manifesting as countless patterns or matrices of action ('matter'). From the point of view of The Awareness Principle, awareness is not awareness of actual realities alone, but also of potential realities. Potential realities however, have reality only 'subjectively' - in awareness itself rather than in actuality. These subjective potentialities do not merely exist as imaginary possibilities however, but as infinite potential shapes, patterns and qualities *of* awareness or subjectivity - infinite potential beings, 'consciousnesses' or 'subjectivities'. 'Energy' in its true and root meaning is the autonomous power of actualisation of these potentialities – something possible only through the awareness of them. Together with the scientific notion of 'space' as a potential source of limitless 'free' energy goes the project, pursued by many great scientific minds, of creating machines to 'tap' this energy as a source of power. The Awareness Principle (TAP) on the other hand, explains how everything that exists in the universe constantly 'TAPS' from a hidden power source behind it - a power of action that is not some mysterious new form of energy or matter but is nothing other than Awareness as such in the form of its aetheric spatiality – Akasha. Each of us experiences this aspect of The Awareness Principle - and realises the idea of free 'space energy' - each time we feel revitalised by taking a walk outdoors, however short. For no matter how little bodily breathing or 'exercise' is involved we are breathing awareness of a wider space - and tapping fresh vitality or 'power of action' from the very air of awareness itself.

The Awareness Principle and Western Psychology

The Awareness Principle is an important basic principle of psychology, yet one that is ignored in contemporary Western understandings of 'consciousness', as well as in 'counselling' and 'psychotherapy' as they have developed in the West. That is because Western psychology has not yet even recognised, as Eastern philosophy has long done, a most basic axiom of the principle itself, namely that awareness as such is quite distinct from its psychological contents, that as 'pure consciousness' it transcends everything we are conscious or aware of. In contrast to the principles of different forms of Western psychology, psychotherapy and psychological counselling, including so-called 'cognitive' therapies, The Awareness Principle does not focus on specific *contents* of consciousness (thoughts, emotions, life event etc.) but rests on a Fundamental Distinction between all such contents – all elements of our experience - and the larger space or 'field' of awareness in which they arise. Recognising this Fundamental Distinction allows us to make a Fundamental Choice – between focussing on, identifying with and thus binding ourselves to the contents of our consciousness - or identifying with the pure awareness of them, an awareness that is innately free of thought, emotional charge or any element of our experience.

The Awareness Principle recognises the transcendental character of awareness. It also recognises its 'immanent' character – that awareness is also present within each and everything we are aware of. Awareness transcends everything we are aware of – for it is the ultimate source of all that is. Precisely because it is the source of everything however, everything we are aware of is also an awareness in its own right. Every sensation, feeling or thought, every physical or mental symptom is itself an awareness of something beyond itself – for example a situation or something going on in another person.

A bodily sensation such as hotness or sweating is not just something we are aware of. It is also our way of sensing something beyond it – for example the heat of the Sun or something we are anxious about. Similarly any feeling is not just something we are aware of. Instead it is a 'pre-reflective' or 'unformulated' awareness of something or someone beyond itself (a relationship, situation or life question for example) just as a thought may be a reflective and formulated awareness of something beyond it. Even a bodily symptom or mental state such as anxiety or depression for example, is not just something we are aware of. Nor is it a life 'problem' in itself. Instead the symptom is itself a bodily awareness of a life problem.

The Awareness Principle and the 'Unconscious'

Most of today's high priests of biological psychiatry are quite unable to step outside the box of today's scientific culture. They regard Freudian thinking and traditional psychoanalysis as 'unscientific' because they are not 'evidence-based' or make use of 'unverifiable constructs' such as *ego, id, libido, the unconscious* etc. In this way however, they expose their *unawareness* of the historical evolution of their *own* most basic concepts - failing to recognise that these themselves are no less unverifiable constructs and far from 'evidence-based'. Thus even physical-scientific concepts such as 'quanta', 'matter waves', 'dark energy', not to mention its most basic concept – the concepts of 'matter' and 'energy' as such - are no less 'unverifiable constructs' than what Freud termed 'the unconscious'. As Martin Heidegger remarked, "physics as physics" - as a theoretical framework - is not itself the object of any possible physical experiment. Similarly there is no possible scientific experiment that could prove the 'verifiability' of the modern-scientific *concept* of 'energy' or show its superiority to earlier concepts, not least earlier historical understandings of the word 'energy' itself – long since forgotten and altered and distorted in the scientific march of 'progress'. The same applies to the diagnostic categories of so-called 'scientific' psychiatry most of which are mere arbitrarily constructed labels for groups of vaguely defined symptoms.

The fact that scientific terms are constructs – labels that no experiment can verify – does not mean that they lack meaning. Freud's concept of the unconscious may be no more verifiable than those of so-called 'hard science' but that does not mean it does not have meaning or point to something real ('pointing to' being the very meaning of the German verb *bedeuten* – 'to mean'). Freud compared consciousness to a torch light. Yet every act of using that torch light to single out and focus on something in the larger field of our awareness, risks blinding us to that field. It is comparable to pointing a torch in the dark – reducing our visual awareness field to what the spotlight of the torch happens to be pointed at and focussed on. Freud was well aware however that meaning has not only to do with some particular element or event in everyday or dream experience that is present in the foreground of our awareness – or that we point at, focus on and single out with the torchlight of our consciousness. Instead he was acutely aware of there being a larger historical, social and personal context to all such singled-out elements or events, and of the way in which the deeper meaning of single elements or events has to do with this larger context. Yet instead of distinguishing our torch-like focal awareness from a quite different type of 'holistic' or 'field' awareness, he stuck to an identification of consciousness with focal awareness – his own favourite tool and still the most respectably scientific tool of investigation. He can be compared to a forensic scientist rigorously searching the psyche in the dark with his torch, always aware that there was something *more* to be seen than what the torch was currently illuminating - something that could therefore provide new material for 'analysis' and add new dimensions of meaning of the visible. Thus he was forever pointing the acute analytic torchlight of his own consciousness in new and different directions, in order to provide clues to these additional dimensions of meaning. The problem is that no matter how serious and rigorous his scientific 'searching in the dark' was, he did not believe in the possibility of simply *switching on the light* – thus illuminating the entire room and entire field of awareness within which all things stand out in their immediate interrelatedness. Consequently the Freudian concept of 'the unconscious' maintained connotations of something innately dark, mysterious and potentially threatening, just as its counterpart - the conscious 'ego' - was seen as the holder and controller of the torch of consciousness, albeit an ego fearful of aiming it in particular directions.

Freud's concept of the 'unconscious' arose from his identification of consciousness *as such* with *focal awareness*. The idea of consciousness having a holistic or field character – the concept of *field awareness* - was therefore replaced by the notion of an 'unconscious', comparable to a room permanently in the dark unless its invisible contents emerged in our dreams, thus also enabling the waking ego to turn its analytic torchlight on them. Freud's identification of consciousness with focal awareness however, was no mere personal failing – for it served the purpose of revealing the identification of 'consciousness' in Western culture purely with the ego and ego-awareness. Yet ego awareness is precisely a type of *focal* awareness which, in restricting itself to singling out specific elements of experience *loses* awareness of their overall field or context of emergence - and of other elements in that field - thus making itself 'unaware' or 'unconscious' of them. Yet even from the point of view of physics, what any 'thing' *is* is determined by the larger field or context of its emergence – 'emergence' being the root meaning of the Greek word *physis* from which the modern term 'physics' derives.

Freud's pioneering work was not indeed a 'discovery' of the unconscious - as if it were some 'thing in itself'. Yet by introducing the notion of 'the unconscious' he pointed to a significant connection between ego-centred, focal awareness on the one hand and the 'unconscious' *memory* or *forgetting* that results from lack of field awareness on the other. For if consciousness is nothing more than focal awareness, a mere torch light capable of illuminating or singling out only one thing or group of things at a time, then it is only natural that when we switch its focus to some other thing, the first thing can easily be forgotten. Lacking a broader field awareness we cannot retain simultaneous awareness of all the elements within it, thus making them appear as 'unconsciously' forgotten elements. And since ego-awareness is like a torchlight used in the dark – without the light switched on - it is only natural that this field-awareness should be felt by the ego, and seen by Freud, as something intrinsically dark or 'unconscious' – something difficult to *fully* bring to light, and tending to conceal repressed elements of the soul or psyche within it. The dark Freudian unconscious then, became a secular equivalent of the religious concept of Hell. Significantly, this is a word sharing roots with the German adjective 'hell' – meaning 'bright'. How then, does the light of awareness come - through a process of forgetting - to take the form of something dim, dark or 'hellish' of which the ego is unaware or 'unconscious'?

In 'The Singularity of Awareness' Michael Kosok describes the process as a four-stage one:

"We all single out a given … element of interest, playing, learning, testing, ignoring its context and even childishly forgetting it by dismissal, if only for a moment, like a game of 'make believe'. But then the simple act of ignoring too often leads to a state of ignorance where we "forget that we have forgotten", as the psychologist R.D. Laing so astutely observed. We can see in this simple scenario the beginning of three steps in seed form. The first is fragmentation, which makes possible the activity of 'singling' out elements from a background – to highlight them into view for contrast or comparisons. This may not seem like any kind of serious fragmentation, but it lays the foundation for shifting to focal awareness in contrast to holistic awareness."

"It is interesting to note that in a recent study where Western children were compared to Oriental children in their mode of perception of a pond of fish, Western students immediately focussed on the biggest fish, and only later took into consideration some contextual material. The Eastern students, from the very beginning, described the ongoing holistic pattern of fishes, water and other elements as a singular structure, in which the biggest fish were not that outstanding."

"After fragmentation, then comes dissociation, which means that an act of ignoring takes place, and what is now a background ... becomes dissociated from what is focussed on as the important foreground and takes on a minimal value. [Memory] may return in a dream state, or it may simply return within direct awareness. But now the third state enters and this is where dissociation becomes hardened. It is where we not only forget but "forget that we have forgotten" and, as a result, a genuine delusion sets in – together with covering illusions ... This is where one begins not to be aware directly – face-to-face – but through a glass darkly."

The 'darkness' lies in perceiving a world of separated or singled out elements or structured complexes of such elements – yet without any sense of the singular unifying light that first brings them to light and embraces them all. This, in terms of many religious philosophies is the 'divine light'. It is understood both in tantric metaphysics and in terms of The Awareness Principle as the very light *of* awareness itself, a light without which 'no-thing' – including light itself – could appear or 'come to light' within awareness.

"Remember what the true 'glasses of divine light' see: each distinction and *particular* form, term or being is fully distinct and unique throughout the entire field of presence, without conflict. However it requires the appropriate centre of vision (the 'eye that is single') to see and experience this Sacred universe of light and love as a truly awesome universe beyond captivity, expressing ranges from the deepest states of tenderness to the highest states of ecstasy. The 'eye that is single' is the *depth* of awareness that goes beyond the dim awareness that is glued to the shallow surface of existence in which all that happens is defined through opposition."

The Awareness Principle is the simple recognition that awareness cannot – in principle – be reduced to a property or function of any thing, being or self that we are aware of. Freud saw 'the unconscious' as the private property of the individual psyche. Jung sensed something wrong here, and thus introduced the notion of a 'collective unconscious'. Neither recognised the essential 'mistake' at stake here, one long recognised in Indian philosophy, namely the basic veiling delusion ('Anavamala') that awareness can in any way be seen as private property - whether of the individual or 'collective' psyche. There is no more any such thing as 'my' unconscious, 'yours' or 'ours' than there is any such thing as 'my' awareness, 'yours' or 'ours'. On the contrary, awareness itself and as such is that singular reality which both manifests itself in infinite individual and collective forms. It is awareness that individualises or 'individuates' itself, just as it is awareness that collectivises itself in the form of shared cultural identities and 'archetypes'. Awareness is also that 'eye that is single' – the 'third eye'. In practice, Freud – perhaps even more than Jung - was aware of what he himself could only explain as a type of direct 'telepathic' communication between the unconscious of the patient and that of the psychoanalyst. Yet the very question concerning the scientific verifiability of 'telepathy' begs the question. For the question is already based on a pre-conception that awareness or subjectivity, whether in the form of 'consciousness', the 'preconscious' or 'subconscious', or 'the unconscious', is the private property of localised individual subjects, bounded by the individual psyche or their physical body. In contrast, The Awareness Principle recognises the non-local or field character of awareness, and thus also its *innate* function as a communicative medium.

By its very nature, the nature of our silent feeling awareness of ourselves and of others - whether spoken or unspoken - automatically communicates *to* others, whether or not they shine the torchlight of their ego-awareness on it and are therefore 'conscious' of it. Since as beings we are not separate in the first place, but instead inseparable, individual expressions of a singular field of awareness, there is no need of any mechanism of telepathic transmission between individuals to explain the innate inner communication of awareness that occurs between individuals. Being the very medium *out of which* our most private sense of ourselves and others first arises, awareness is also the medium through which it constantly communicates.

The so-called 'conscious' mind is not more but *less* conscious – less aware - than this 'unconscious'. The mystery of 'the unconscious' can thus never be unraveled unless we understand its depths not as depths of 'unawareness' but of *awareness* - not the narrow *focal* awareness of the ego, but all that remains unaware or 'unconscious' for the ego through this narrowness of focus – 'narrowness' (German *Enge*) being, interestingly, both the root meaning of the word anxiety (German *Angst*) and its real-life foundation. It is the ego that 'keeps itself in the dark' and therefore 'anxious' - never switching on the light of field awareness but instead constantly pursuing its own ever-more detailed probings and 'analyses', whether personal or scientific, of what its torchlight focuses on in the dark.

In contrast, 'enlightenment' means 'turning on' the light of awareness. Doing so, we experience the 'unconscious' not as something dim or murky but *as* a larger field of illumination – a *superconsciousness* transcending the narrow ego boundaries of ordinary consciousness. Along with the experience of this 'superconsciousness' goes the experience of a *superself.* This is not a Freudian-style 'superego' made up of internalized social mores or parental judgements. Indeed it is not any self we can be aware *of.* Instead it is that eternal self or 'I' – and that single 'eye' – that does not 'have' or 'possesses' but *is* awareness. This eternal, universal and divine self, the 'Atman' in Indian terms, is one we can come to know only by *being* it – by 'being awareness'. It was named in the very first of the 'Shiva Sutras' – the scriptural aphorism or 'threads' (Sutra) that form the revelatory foundation of the tantric metaphysics and psychology of Kashmir

Shaivism. For the Sutra reads simply – 'Chaitanya-atman' – which can be translated as 'Awareness-Being-Self' or 'Awareness *is* the Self'. It is our *unconsciousness of this truth* – the truth that awareness is not only the essence of 'the unconscious' but also the essence of 'self' - that is the basis of all theories of 'the unconscious' and the key to their deeper significance.

The flip side of 'un-consciousness' is a sustained awareness of the 'un-', of all that ordinary normal consciousness, with its narrowed focus, tends to consistently ignore, forget and in turn forget that it has forgotten, identifying its own truly 'unconscious' state of *unawareness* as 'ordinary' or 'normal' consciousness - and even taking this ordinary consciousness as a benchmark both of mental health and 'scientific' knowledge. This is the basic error that Freud challenged, unlike today's haughty scientists and psychiatrists who remain stuck in it. Since his time however, the latter have persisted in their search for a material or biological or evolutionary basis for 'consciousness', whilst never pausing to consider the basic paradox - made explicit through The Awareness Principle – namely that since it is a singular *field* of subjectivity and not some subject or object within that field, awareness cannot be explained by any thing or collection of things that we single out and focus on within that field - including the human brain and its 'hard-wiring'. The aim of articulating The Awareness Principle will be fulfilled even if all it does is to show how so-called 'hard' science' has, in reality, the weakest and least solid of philosophical foundations, thus undermining its attacks, not only on Freud and psychoanalysis, but on a whole range of alternative scientific and spiritual world views with a far longer tradition and far firmer foundations – albeit long forgotten ones.

THE THEOLOGY OF AWARENESS

Awareness as 'Universal Consciousness'

I hail that Universal Consciousness [*Vijnana-Bhairava/ Shivachaitanya*] of which everything and everyone is a unique portion and expression, individual yet indivisible from the whole!

The Universal Consciousness is not awareness *of* things but awareness *as such*. It is not 'yours' or 'mine' but the essence of the Divine, a consciousness universal and unbounded.

'God' is not a supreme being 'with' consciousness, nor does any person or being 'have' or 'possess' consciousness as its private property. Instead God *is* consciousness.

All individual beings and persons are bounded portions, expressions and personifications of the Universal Consciousness that *is* God.

The bodily boundaries of individual consciousness no more separate it from the Universal Consciousness than does the skin of a fish separate it from the ocean.

Our own skin is a permeable boundary, one that does not separate us from the air around us but unites us with it - breathing that air. Were our skin a sealed boundary we would die from lack of air.

In essence, what is called the 'unconscious' (ucs) *is* the Universal Consciousness (UCS).

The 'ego' or 'conscious' mind, on the other hand, is not more but *less* conscious than *this* 'unconscious' - it is a contraction of the Universal Consciousness within the Universal Consciousness.

Many people speak of consciously 'creating' their reality. In truth it is their 'unconscious' in the Freudian sense that 'creates' their reality - constantly seeking ways to express all that escapes the *contracted* awareness of their 'conscious' mind, and doing so in ways the conscious ego remains unaware of.

If your sole motto is 'I create my reality', you have not yet asked who or what this 'I' is. It is not the conscious mind or ego, but all that remains unconscious to it through its limited and contracted awareness.

In reality there is only ONE creative source of all realities and of the ego or 'I' itself - the Universal Consciousness.

The Universal Consciousness has the innate power or capacity (*Shakti*) to give form to itself - manifest, individualise and personify itself in infinite potential forms. Thus it not only transcends and surrounds but pervades all its manifestations – all beings.

The Universal Consciousness is truly transcendent and immanent – surrounding and pervading all things.

Everything actual is a form taken *by* the Universal Consciousness *within* the Universal Consciousness. There can be nothing outside the Universal Consciousness as there can be nothing 'outside' space or 'before' time.

"We are inside God." Jane Roberts. Everything exists within the Universal Consciousness – within God.

Being *inseparable* from the The Universal Consciousness as a whole every being *is* that Consciousness as a whole, is 'God'.

Being a *distinct* portion of The Universal Consciousness as a whole everything is at the same time a unique expression of it - 'a god'.

God is not a person. Yet all persons are both God and gods – being both portions of the Universal Consciousness *as a whole*, and individualised personifications of it.

God, though not a person, is thus a 'multiperson' – every person being a personification or face (*persona*) of the Universal Consciousness.

The Universal Consciousness is no mere 'state' of 'cosmic consciousness' to be evolved by or attained by individual human beings. It is the divine source and innermost nature of all beings, all individualised consciousness.

As individualised consciousnesses we experience ourselves as bodies 'in' space. In contrast, the Universal Consciousness experiences itself in the same way that space might experience both itself and the bodies in it – as that which both surrounds and pervades them.

If we can identify with the entire space around us, and experience our own bodies as it does, as *within* it and not just 'in' it, we *are* identifying with the Universal Consciousness.

Space and time as such *are* the primary expression of the Universal Consciousness in our space-time reality.

The Universal Consciousness is an infinite 'time-space' or 'time-sphere' of awareness embracing all realities – past, present and future, actual and potential.

Ordinary consciousness is a narrow, focussed awareness, like a torchlight in a dark room. The Universal Consciousness is like light pervading space in a lightened room or sunny day.

- Light [Prakasha] is the light of the Universal Consciousness – the Light of Awareness.
- Space [Akasha] is the spacious, all-pervasive aether of the Universal Consciousness.
- Air [Prana] is the immanent vitality of the Universal Consciousness.
- Water is the oceanic fluidity of the Universal Consciousness.
- Fire is the transformative power of the Universal Consciousness.
- Matter is the formative matrix of the Universal Consciousness.
- Planets are materialised planes of the Universal Consciousness.
- Bodies are embodiments of the Universal Consciousness.
- Suns are radiant centres of the Universal Consciousness.

Shiva/Bhairava are traditional names for the Universal Consciousness in its aspect as *pure awareness*.

Shakti/Bhairavi are traditional names for the Universal Consciousness in its aspect as *pure power* of manifestation.

From Mono- and Polytheism to 'Nootheism'

- **Theism** is the belief that God exists as a BEING.

- **Monotheism** is the belief that God is ONE supreme BEING separate from the world and other BEINGS.

- **Polytheism** is the belief in a plurality of Gods, each of which is a divine or trans-human BEING.

- **Hentheism** (from the Greek 'hen' meaning 'one') is the belief that God is the ONENESS of all beings or 'BEING' as such.

- **Henotheism** is a form of polytheism resting on the belief in one supreme BEING or God ruling over all other gods and beings.

- **Pantheism** (from the Greek word 'pan' meaning 'all') is the belief that God IS the world - is ALL BEINGS.

- **Atheism**, strictly speaking, is not disbelief in God. It is disbelief in the existence of God as a BEING.

- **Panatheism** ('Buddhism') is the belief that NO BEINGS exist, because everything is in a constant state of BECOMING.

- **Panentheism** (from the Greek words 'pan' and 'en', meaning 'all' and 'in') is the belief that all BEINGS dwell IN God, and that God dwells IN all BEINGS.

- **Nootheism** (from the Greek 'noos', meaning 'awareness') is a form of 'panentheism' that identifies God with the awareness IN which all BEINGS constantly 'BE-COME' or 'COME-TO-BE', in which they all 'dwell', and which also dwells in them all.

'Shiva', 'Shaivism' and 'Nootheology'

'Nootheism' is a new term, which names the fundamental religious principle or 'God-concept' of 'The Awareness Principle'. This is not a principle that negates those of other religions, but one that can actually encompass them all. The religious philosophy of Kashmir Shaivism showed that this was possible. For it both derived from, incorporated and transcended many traditional forms of Indian religious theism, polytheism, henotheism, hentheism and pantheism – just as it also incorporated and transcended Buddhist panatheism, and thus pointed the way to a new philosophical understanding of atheism. It did this through its presentation and reinterpretation of the nature of the traditional Hindu god SHIVA. 'Shaivism' means simply the religion of Shiva. Yet in the tradition of Kashmir Shaivism the name 'Shiva' is 'overcoded' – denoting and connoting much more than was previously meant by this name, and comprehending much more through it. For this is a tradition which understood itself as 'catholic' in the most literal sense – embracing all the God-concepts and practices of other faiths within the higher truth constituted by a fundamental 'nootheistic' understanding of God – the understanding that 'God *is* Awareness' and 'Awareness is God'.

What the name 'Shiva' – seemingly that of a single god among others – a actually connotes within the metaphysical theology, philosophy or 'theosophy' of Kashmir Shaivism includes all of the following denotations:

The nootheistic Shiva - God as identical with awareness (*noos/chit*)

The panentheistic Shiva – God as that awareness in which all things dwell and which dwells in all things.

The (pan-)atheistic Shiva – God as that pure *awareness* of being that is not a being of any sort - even a 'Supreme Being'.

The pantheistic Shiva – God as an awareness which is everything and every being.

The henotheistic Shiva – the Shiva that 'rules' over other gods precisely because it is not a god in the sense of a single divine being among others.

The hentheistic or monistic Shiva – God as the monistic character of awareness, its singularity or Oneness.

The polytheistic Shiva – God (Shiva) as awareness in all its infinite personifications and 'powers' (Shaktis), as all gods and goddesses, and as the godliness of every being.

The monotheistic Shiva – awareness as the singular, divine creative *source* of each and every being.

The theistic Shiva – God as the singular awareness personified by a single god.

Awareness as Unified Field Theology

Awareness is not something that dwells 'in' us, bounded by our bodies. We ourselves dwell *in* awareness in the same way that objects exist in space. Both the physical space we sense around our bodies and the psychic spaces we sense within them are subjective spaces – the spaces of awareness within which we are aware of things and without which we could be aware of nothing. *We exist in awareness* – inner and outer – in the same way that the elements of our outer and inner world can only be experienced in spaces – inner and outer. All space being subjective, there is essentially only one space from which we emerge and in which we exist, an unbounded space of divine awareness. Christianity understood this 'Awareness Principle' through the metaphor of 'The Kingdom' that is both outside us and inside us. Buddhism understood it through the principle that form and the formlessness of space are inseparable. Kashmir Shaivism understood it through the principle of *Shiva-Shakti*. *Shiva* – the unbounded, bodiless space of divine awareness (*akula*) in which every body exists, and which embraces the totality (*kula*) of bodies that make up the "embodied cosmos" (Muller-Ortega) or *Shakti* of *Shiva*.

All awareness is awareness of things sensuous, bodily. Even the most abstract of thoughts has its own 'body' – its own sensuous shape and form. But the awareness of things bodily, including our own bodies, is not itself anything bodily, but is something essentially bodiless – like the formlessness of space. How then do bodily things form themselves in the first place? Because formless awareness that we perceive as empty space is not in fact empty but is a fullness of formative *potentials*. Such potentials – all potentials – only exist in awareness, and do so as potential shapes and forms of awareness. Formless awareness gives birth to form from these potentials. As the formlessness of space it shapes itself into bodily forms. *Shakti* is the very power and process of actualisation of these potentials – the bodiless, formless awareness of *Shiva* giving form to itself into countless bodily shapes. We are such bodily shapes of awareness. As such we are not only formed from divine awareness space. We exist in that space as we exist in space itself. And that space exists within us just as we exist within it. We are each a unified space or field of awareness, our bodies a mere boundary between the awareness we exist within and the awareness that exists within us. To perceive an object with awareness is to perceive it in its place - in the surrounding space in which alone it stands out or 'ex-ists'. But look around at people – people you know and people on the street – and you will see something different. You will see from their bodies – indeed from the very look on their face - that they do not sense themselves as existing *in* awareness, just as they do in *space*. They feel their awareness as something that exists only within their body's fleshly boundaries – where even there it may be contracted to the narrowest of spaces in their heads. Spiritual 'enlightenment' is nothing but the *decontraction* of the sensed awareness space in which we exist and which exists within us – its outer expansion and inward expansion or 'inpansion'. The bounded inner space of awareness was named by the Greek word *psyche*, the Latin *anima*, and the Sanskrit *jiva,* the outer space by the Greek word *pneuma*, the Latin *spiritu*s, and the Sanskrit *akasha*.

Every religion has its sacred places and spaces. Buildings are erected in such places to mark out and bound the sacred spaces within them. The word 'temple' (Latin *templum*) means such a consecrated inner space. A building such as a temple is also a shaping of space, one which lends a specific quality both to the space within it and to the space of the landscape or cityscape in which it is set. The dome of St. Peter lends a different quality to the spaces within and around it to that of a Gothic cathedral, a Buddhist *stupa* or a Hindu temple. The same principle applies to the objects set within such holy spaces. They also, like the objects in our own homes, lend a specific quality to the space in which they are set and have their place. Is there anything at all that can truly unite all religions, given the quite *different* quality of the awareness spaces they shape in such specific ways - through their languages and images, rituals and sacred places? The only thing that *could* unite them in essence would be a *unified field theology* of awareness - one which recognises the embrace of divine awareness in space as such. The essential religious philosophy or 'theosophy' of The Awareness Principle, like that of 'Kashmir Shaivism', is such a unified field theology – comprehending the unity of outer and inner awareness space, of 'The Kingdom' outside and inside, of *pneuma* and *psyche,* of formlessness and form, of potentiality (*dynamis*) and its actualisation (*energeia*), of a*kula* and *kula,* of *Shiva* and *Shakti.* Unified field theology, by virtue of offering a unified field theory of awareness and its expression as energy and matter, also unifies spirituality and science, psychology and physics. But being a unified field theory of awareness the heart of such a unified field theology must be *unified field awareness* as such. Through The Awareness Principle each individual can come to experience themselves as existing within divine awareness as within space. Similarly, they can come to experience that divine awareness within them - as their body's very inwardness of soul. By uniting the spatial fields of their awareness with one another, they can not only realise a state of decontracted and divine awareness for themselves - they can also unite their own fields of awareness with those of others.

Neither theological liberalism and heterodoxy nor conservative orthodoxy and 'inquisitions' bear any relation to the type of genuine meditative *inquiry* required to research, rethink and refind the common source and essence of religious practices and symbols - in all their different historical and cultural forms. This common source and essence can only be found in the direct experience of unified field awareness. What the world requires now is a *new world religion* of the sort hoped for by Hermann Hesse, one based on a *newly thought* theology. This can only be a *unified field theology* which, whatever its historic roots, is based on a renewed experience of the divine as the *foundational* and *unified field awareness* in which all worlds arise and all beings dwell - as it dwells within them. The true body of the human being is a *unified field body* of awareness uniting three fields of awareness – a *field of exteriority* manifest as our awareness of the physical space around us, a field of interiority which we feel as the spacious inwardness of our own soul - and the field of *unbounded interiority* into which our own inwardness of soul leads. This field of unbounded interiority is also the *all-surrounding* field that constitutes the *soul world* as such – that which lies *behind* all that we perceive in the exterior space around us. It is *within* this field of unbounded and all-surrounding 'interiority' that all seemingly 'exterior' spaces of awareness - all space-time worlds – first open up. Our unified field body is the singular *field-boundary* of awareness uniting all three fields. Yet precisely *as* this very boundary it is itself essentially boundless – a *unified field awareness*.

Unified Field Awareness & the Unified Field Body

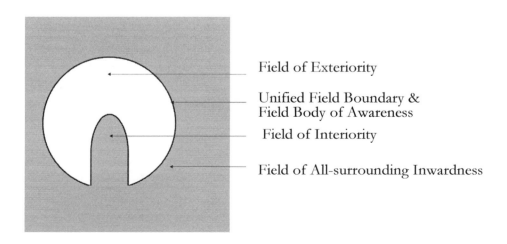

Field of Exteriority

Unified Field Boundary &
Field Body of Awareness

Field of Interiority

Field of All-surrounding Inwardness

Tantra and the Dialectics of Divinity

Though historical scholars distinguish 'Shakta' (goddess worshipping) and 'Shaiva' schools of tantrism, in the tantric tradition these schools are 'non-dual'. 'God' is essentially neither masculine nor feminine and yet also both. Instead God is 'Shiva-Shakti' - the eternal procreation of God as a divine couple, uniting the divine masculine ('Shiva' as *pure awareness*) with the divine feminine ('Shakti' as *pure power* of manifestation).

Understood in the light of The Awareness Principle, 'Shiva' is in its *field* character. 'Shakti' is the presencing or actualisation of any being or body, any thing or phenomenon – any identifiable 'element" within the field of awareness that is Shiva. Field and elements, Shiva and Shakti, are inseparable – the field being a field *of* elements and all elements being elements *of* a field.

An 'element' within a field can be likened to an object in space or circle on a blank sheet. Each such element is defined just as much by the space around it – the 'transcendental' field within which it emerges (Shiva) as by the 'immanent' space or field of awareness it bounds and contains.

The circle as circle is neither Shiva nor Shakti, field nor element. It is a dynamic boundary state of element *and* field, circle and surrounding space – it is *Shiva-Shakti*.

'Shaivism' cannot be opposed in principle to 'Shaktism'. For it is the understanding that every element (Shakti) emerging within a field is a *self-manifestation* of that field and therefore of Shiva. Yet since the 'transcendental' field is made up of and inseparable from the elements that emerge within it, Shiva also cannot exist without Shakti.

Yet the dynamic relation of awareness and beings, field and elements, Shiva and Shakti – is an even more deeply reciprocal or 'dialectical' one. For understood dialectically, the inter-relation of fields of awareness and elements of experience is a 'dialectic matrix' (Michael Kosok) or interweave ('tantra') made up of nine distinct but inseparable aspects:

1. **The field as field (Shiva)**
2. **The elements as elements (Shakti)**
3. **The immanent field within each element (Shiva within Shakti)**
4. **The elements within each field (Shakti within Shiva)**
5. **The field as a field of elements (Shiva as Shakti)**
6. **The elements as elements of a field (Shakti as Shiva)**
7. **The relation of field and elements (Shiva-Shakti) as a self-relation of the field to itself mediated by the elements within it (Shiva-Shakti as Shiva)**
8. **The relation of elements and field as a self-relation of the elements to themselves through the field that they constitute (Shiva-Shakti as Shakti)**
9. **The entire 'transcendental' field of elements (Shiva-Shakti) as something 'immanent' within each and every element of the field (Shakti-Shiva).**

Within this dialectical perspective, Shiva and Shakti are not *separable* gods, beings or identities that exist 'in' multiple relationships to one another. Instead they are elements *of* a singular dynamic relation: Shiva-Shakti. This singular dynamic relation is the universe understood tantrically - as the sexual union ('Maithuna') of a divine couple ('Yamala'). Paradoxically however, sexuality *as such* is nothing essentially sexual in the fleshly, bodily sense. Similarly, sexual union *as such* – as union or 'yoga' - is neither masculine nor feminine but 'beyond gender'. It is not an *external* relation of *separable* masculine and feminine gods, beings or aspects of divinity. Instead, what we call 'masculine' and 'feminine' are both aspects *of* that dynamic relation we call 'sexual union'. From a truly *tantric* perspective, 'sex' and 'sexual union' are nothing essentially physical or human. Instead the universe as such and as a whole *is* 'sex', understood as the 'dialectics of divinity', a dynamic weave of *pure awareness* on the one hand, and its *pure power* of manifestation in the form of identifiable things, beings or elements of experience on the other hand. This 'weave' is a root meaning of 'tantra' itself.

Awareness and the 'Doctrine of Recognition'

"I who have obtained, thanks to the benevolence of the Supreme Lord, the benefits that derive from being His servant – a state it is very difficult to achieve – being ashamed of my solitary success, shall by the method that will here be described, enable the whole of humanity to recognise their Lord, in order to gain my complete fulfilment through the attainment also by them of the Supreme Reality."

Introduction to the *Ishvarapratyabhijnakarika* of Utpaladeva, as

translated by Raffaele Torrella, Motilal Banarsidass, 1994

What follows is an articulation of The Awareness Principle in terms of a new and original exposition of the Shaivist 'Doctrine of Recognition' (*Pratyabhijna*) as first expounded by Somananda and Utpaladeva, and expressed here in the traditional form of verse stanzas or 'karika':

The pure radiant light (*Prakasha*) of the ultimate awareness that is the 'Supreme Reality' *(Anuttara)* is what first brings the colourations of all things to light out of colourless darkness, that womb of inexhaustible potentiality that is the Great Goddess (*Mahadevi*).

The pure radiant light of the ultimate awareness is that which, by pervading all things, allows all things to experience and revel in their unique individual tints or colourations.

Without the pure, radiant light of the ultimate awareness to illuminate its individual colouration, nothing would be aware of being that colour - nothing would be aware of being.

The being of all things is their individuality – comparable to a unique colouration of awareness.

The radiant light of the ultimate awareness is that which brings to light, pervades and shines through the infinitely differentiated unique tints or colouration of all things.

Like 'white' light which contains all colours, the ultimate awareness *recognises* itself in all its infinite colourations, in all beings.

It recognises itself not just *as* those individual colourations or beings however, but as that pure 'colourless' light which is not bound to any colour. For only a pure 'full spectrum light' can be filtered or reflected as any *specific* colour or wavelength of light.

The self-recognition (*Vimarsha*) of the pure, radiant light of awareness (*Prakasha*) in all its infinite hues is what alone gives everything an awareness of its own individual hue - an awareness of its *individual* being or 'selfhood'.

The self-recognition of the pure, radiant light of awareness in its own *absolute purity* however - as that which alone allows it to shine and manifest in all its infinitely differentiated hues - is its *supreme self-hood* or 'I-consciousness'.

The recognition by all things of the pure light of awareness as that which alone *allows* them to shine in their individual hues is their own true *self-recognition* - their recognition of that pure light as their divine 'I' or self.

The recognition *by* all things of the pure light of awareness as their divine self is at the same time the self-recognition *of* that light itself.

'Our' process of coming to *recognise* our selves as identical with the supreme 'I'-consciousness or selfhood of the ultimate awareness, is also *its self-recognition* – albeit a self-recognition whose process is already and eternally *complete*.

Anuttara, the absolute or ultimate reality, is not God in the sense of a being or self 'with' awareness. It does not 'have' or 'possess' awareness but *is* awareness – ultimate, absolute and unbounded.

The very *essence* of awareness however, is its *recognitive* character, its character of recognising itself in all things, recognising them as manifestations and reflections of its light.

The recognitive character of awareness is Shiva-Shakti, the relation of inseparable distinction between pure awareness (Shiva) and its self-recognition in all that there is to be aware *of* (Shakti).

The Self-recognition of Shiva is itself a Supreme Shakti - the Shakti by which awareness experiences itself as the Supreme Self.

Thus, whilst the "Supreme Reality" or ultimate awareness called *Anuttara* is not 'God' but 'Godhead', it is nevertheless inseparable from its own 'Godhood'. For its 'Divine Self-Recognition' is a recognitive awareness of 'itself' *as* 'God' or "Supreme Lord".

The self-recognition of the light of the ultimate awareness in and as all things *is* the recognition of its own 'Selfhood', 'Divinity', 'Godhood' or 'Lordship'.

That is why 'The Doctrine of Recognition' is a doctrine of 'Divine Self-Recognition'.

The Doctrine of Recognition is also innately self-reflexive, being *itself* the recognition that both thoughts and things themselves are reflections and manifestations of the light of a Divine Awareness - which can thus recognise itself in them all.

Any doctrine is necessarily couched in discriminatory verbal concepts (*Vikalpa*). Yet verbal concepts (*Vikalpa*) are not just a form of 'reflective' or 'reflected' awareness - the mental mirror or reflection of a non-verbal and a-conceptual awareness (*Nirvikalpa*).

Instead, each concept *is* an awareness itself - a *recognitive awareness* of something. Words and concepts are, in themselves, the *recognition* of a *wordless, a-conceptual awareness.*

Thus the verbal thought or 'judgement' that 'I am now walking' is not merely the mental reflection in words of a wordless awareness of walking. Instead the mental words and intellectual judgement are themselves a *recognition* of that wordless awareness - in the form of a *recognitive judgement.*

Since the *recognitive awareness* of all things is identical with the *self-recognition* of the ultimate awareness in and through all things, it is *recognitive awareness as such* that constitutes our unity with the divine.

Since every verbal concept *is* a recognitive awareness, the greater the discrimination, differentiation and refinement of awareness in words and concepts, the more deeply we are lead into an experience of pure, wordless and a-conceptual awareness.

In particular, the more refined our concept is of the *recognitive character* of awareness, the more this *conceptual awareness* will itself transform itself into a pure, *a-conceptual experience* of Divine Self-Recognition.

Therefore the doctrine of 'Divine Self-Recognition' is both *means and end* – being an expression of its truth, which, if fully refined and understood, is at the same time an experience of that truth and no mere 'means' to such an experience. The doctrine of Divine Self-Recognition, being itself a *medium* of Divine Self-Recognition, is thus no mere artificially constructed *human* doctrine, but rather both the human revelation and human realisation of its own Divine Truth.

"… only the foolish strive to establish or deny the Lord." *Utpaladeva*

Thus re-cognised, the doctrine of recognition transcends the duality between understanding the divine (*Shiva*) as an absolute subject that is 'Lord' or 'God' ('monistic theism') or as a 'Godhead' (*Anuttara*) which is nothing but 'absolute subjectivity' - an ultimate, singular, non-theistic awareness ('noetic absolutism' or 'nootheism') that is at the same time personified in multiple gods ('monistic polytheism').

Human beings too, are in their essence both 'Gods' and 'God' – being *unique portions and personifications* ('Gods') of the ultimate or divine awareness *in its entirety* ('God'). Central to *its* nature therefore, is its innate power to personify itself in countless forms. This being the case, even in its ultimate nature as 'subjectivity without a subject', (*Anuttara*) the Supreme Reality that is 'Divinity' is neither a person nor a purely 'impersonal' Godhead - for it recognises itself in all its personifications.

The Awareness Principle and Advaita

The many original precepts introduced by The Awareness Principle serve to further differentiate it from and refine the comprehensions and concepts of traditional 'non-dual' or 'a-dvaita' philosophy - including Buddhist philosophy and those profound schools of tantric theology and metaphysics known collectively as 'Kashmir Shaivism'. These original precepts are summarised below:

36 Original Precepts of The Awareness Principle

1. **'Consciousness' is not a good translation of the ultimate reality designated in Sanskrit as 'Chit', 'Samvit', 'Shuddhachit', 'Parachit' or 'Shuddhavidya'.** 'Awareness' or 'pure awareness' is a more appropriate term. For if people get lost in thought or emotions, pains or pleasures, in watching TV or playing computer games, in work or domestic chores – then they may be 'conscious' but they are not *aware*. Whenever our consciousness becomes overly focused or fixated on any one thing we are conscious of, we lose awareness. For unlike ordinary 'consciousness', awareness is intrinsically pure or transcendent, transcending any thing we are conscious or aware *of*. Like space it surrounds, pervades and yet remains absolutely distinct from each and every thing within it. Indeed it is the subjective essence of space itself. That is why identification with inner and outer space ('Khechari Mudra') is the key to a new experience of space itself - as an unbounded *field* of awareness transcending anything that we experience within it.

2. **Not helpful and even more misleading is the common Buddhist translation of 'Chit' as 'mind' ('Buddhi') and of awareness with 'mindfulness'.** For *awareness* of mind and mental activity - and of a mental ego or 'I' - is not itself anything mental. Nor is awareness itself the same as 'witnessing' – a term which implies some 'mindful' self or alter-ego 'doing' the witnessing. Buddhist advaita and tantra contradictorily rejects the notion of self and lets it in again through the back door. It does so by failing to see

219

that whilst *awareness of self* cannot - in principle - be the property of any self or ego 'with' awareness (even a 'mindful' or 'witnessing' self) it is nevertheless identical with that divine Self (Atman) which does not 'have' but *is* awareness.

3. **Pure Awareness is not 'emptiness'.** To speak in Buddhist terms of 'the mind's continuous ascertainment of emptiness' is to create a dualism of mind and awareness, to privilege 'mind' over emptiness - and affirm emptiness itself, rather than pure awareness, as absolute. For just as space is both inseparable from and absolutely distinct from all the objects within it, so also is awareness absolutely distinct from all its contents – from all we are aware *of*. It does not therefore need to be 'emptied' of all content to be as clear and pure as the 'empty' space around us - a space whose essence is pure awareness and not mere 'emptiness'.

4. **'God' – the divine - is not a supreme being, self, soul, subject or 'I' that 'has' or 'possesses' awareness.** As 'Shiva', God IS awareness – an awareness that is independent of any being, human or divine – and yet the source of all beings, all individualised consciousnesses. 'I-consciousness', including the supreme selfhood or 'I-consciousness' of Shiva, is a reflective property of pure awareness - not the other way round. 'Shiva' is not a god 'with' awareness or 'with' a self or 'I', but the 'I'-ness *of* that absolute, foundational awareness which *is* 'God'.

5. **To attain a state of 'pure' or 'transcendental' awareness, thought- and sense-free, mind- and body-free - it is not necessary to cease thinking, close our eyes to the sensory world, stop our minds or dis-identify from our bodies.** That is because the simple *awareness* of a thought, since it is not *itself* a thought, is itself *inherently* thought-free, just as the awareness of our minds and bodies is not itself anything mental or bodily - and is therefore something innately mind- and body-free. Similarly, the awareness of a differentiated world of sensations and perceptions is not itself anything sensory or differentiated, but is the undifferentiated, sense-free space in which they stand out or 'ex-ist'. Like space, awareness is inherently 'transcendental' – transcending every thing or thought, feeling or sensation

we experience within it. The light of pure awareness both intensifies our 'delight' in the sensory world but also finds its reflection and recognition in the refined spiritual intellect.

6. **'Pranayama' is not breath 'control' but simply a sustained *awareness* of breathing.** For the moment we lose awareness of the subtle muscular motions of our *breathing* - even if only for a moment - we lose awareness of our bodies as a whole and of all we are experiencing through them, thus losing awareness *per se*. As a result we cannot experience the true nature of *prana* as the very breath, air or 'aether' of awareness as such. *Pranayama* is the bliss of a sustained *breathing of awareness* that comes from a sustained *awareness of breathing*. All the Practices of Awareness that flow from The Awareness Principle follow the same basic *practical principle* – that of passing from awareness of a specific sensory dimension of our experience (our awareness of breath or light, for example) to a *sensual experience of awareness per se* (for example, an experience of the innate light and breath *of* awareness).

7. **Being ('Sat') and Awareness ('Chit') are not equivalent or equiprimordial concepts.** The Awareness Principle recognises awareness itself as the ultimate unsurpassable and primordial reality ('Anuttara'). That is because Being is essentially *awareness* of Being, and, as recognised by Abhinavagupta "The being of all things that exist in awareness in turn depends on awareness." The Awareness Principle, and not The Being Principle, is the implicit inner principle of tantric metaphysics. Yet it is 'The Being Principle' that has formed the basis of all Western metaphysics and philosophy, and tends also to be privileged in the Vedas and Vedantic philosophy.

8. **'Shakti' is not 'energy' in the modern scientific sense.** The modern scientific use of the term 'energy' is a recent invention - promoted in the 19th century by an elite club of scientists called 'The Energeticist Movement' as an empty quantitative abstraction - one that was raised over all tangible, experiential dimensions of reality. Since then it has become a quasi-religious dogma of both modern science and New Age pseudo-science that 'everything is energy'. The 'energy' concept also served the purposes of

imperialist Anglo-American oil interests, justified by the idea of energy as a 'scarce' planetary resource. The word 'energy' is rooted in the Greek verb *energein* – which was not a scientific abstraction but meant simply formative or creative 'action' (like that of a potter forming a pot). 'Shakti' is rooted in the Sanskrit 'Shak' – meaning 'capacity' or 'power' of action. 'Shaktis' are the infinite potentialities of awareness latent within the divine awareness and released by it as autonomous, self-manifesting *powers of action.*

9. **'Kundalini' or 'Kundalini-Shakti' is not an 'energy' coiled up within the physical body.** As 'serpent power' it is nothing less than the fluid coiling motility and shape-shifting power of awareness itself - as symbolised in countless cultures by the serpent or dragon. Nobody can feel the abstraction called 'energy'. What they can feel is the immense potentiality and *powers of action* ('Shakti') immanent in pure awareness ('Shiva').

10. **'Spanda' is not 'energy' in the modern scientific sense.** It is the eternal tension (German 'Spannung') spanning the primordial realms of actuality and potentiality and the oscillation between them - the vibration of the potential *within* the actual that pervades awareness as its immanent power.

11. **The reality of the unsurpassable and divine absolute ('Anuttara') is not identical with either Being or Non-Being, Shiva or Shakti.** Being is actuality. Yet there is more to reality than actuality – namely the reality of all that is potential. Non-Being is not absolute nothingness but simply *non-actuality.* By the same token it is not an empty void but the fullness of *potentiality.* The divine, as absolute awareness, embraces both the realm of the actual (Being) and that of the potential (Non-Being), including all potential beings, souls or individualised consciousnesses. The light of awareness is the great god ('Mahadeva'/'Shiva') that releases these potentialities from the dark womb of potentiality that is the 'great goddess' ('Mahadevi'/'Mahakali').

12. **Shiva (divine awareness) and Shakti (divine power) are equiprimordial aspects of the absolute reality ('Anuttara') which is the essence of divinity as such.** So-called 'Shaiva' and 'Shakta' schools of tantra can thus in no way be opposed or separated. Abhinavagupta's 'Trika' system of tantric

metaphysics recognised divinity in the form of the divine absolute ('Anuttara'), its twin aspects ('Shiva' and 'Shakti') and their dynamic unity - 'Shiva-Shakti'. So despite its association with 'Shaivist' scriptures and traditions ('Shaivagama'), 'Kashmir Shaivism' should not be taken as privileging Shiva over Shakti. As individualisations of the same divine awareness all beings are 'Shiva'. Through their innate power of autonomous self-actualisation they are also 'Shakti'. All beings, as souls or individualised consciousnesses are thus expressions and embodiments of the absolute as Shiva-Shakti. And worship of the divine in its 'Shakta' or 'feminine' aspect is precisely what leads to an experience of its Shaiva or 'masculine' aspect – and vice versa.

13. **Creation is not the activity of Shiva as divine being, agent or creator god.** Nor is Shiva a divine being or 'I' endowed with independent will ('Iccha') or action ('Kriya') in the same way that the ego believes itself to be. Instead Shiva is that pure quiescent non-active awareness which, by its very nature, lets all potential beings be and sets them free – releasing them into their own free, autonomous self-actualisation, through their own innate power of action ('Shakti'). 'Iccha' is not Shiva's 'own' willed activity as divine ego, 'I' or agent. Instead it is the absolutely free, spontaneous *creativity* ('Kriya') latent in, and arising from pure awareness (Shiva) as its innate power of action (Shakti). 'Shakti' is not the power 'of' Shiva, in the sense of belonging to him. Instead Shakti *is* 'the power of Shiva' - without which he would be a mere corpse ('Shava'), and as the divine awareness would be incapable of manifesting all realities.

14. **'Shaivism' and 'Shaktism' are not opposing schools or denominations of Tantrism.** Nor can the *Shiva-Shakti* principle of *Tantra* be equated with the *Yin-Yang* principles of *Taoism*, which in line with Western and Christian patriarchal stereotypes identifies the 'masculine' principle ('Yang') with aggressive action and controlling power, and the feminine ('Yin') with all that is passive. The primordial masculine principle personified by Shiva in the Shaivist tantrism on the other hand, is not associated with aggressive action, let alone *controlling power over action* (itself a form of action) but rather with stillness and *quiescent awareness of action*. The long-standing and still dominant

identification of the 'masculine' with patriarchal power of control over action, expression, experience (indeed over the entire world of manifestation associated tantrically with the divine feminine) constituted a loss of a more primordial understanding of the divine masculine - not as a power *over* action and creation but rather as that universal awareness which first releases the creative power *of* action – the divine-feminine.

15. **Duality ('Dvaita') does not imply *separation* and nor does non-duality or 'monism' imply lack of *distinction* or differentiation.** The Awareness Principle articulates the essential but still implicit or unthought principle of the entire 'Advaita' or 'non-dual' tradition. This is the principle of *inseparable distinction*. Thus the two sides of a coin are neither 'dual' in the sense of being *separate* nor 'non-dual' in the sense of being *indistinct* or lacking differentiation. Instead they are both dual in the sense of being distinct and at the same time 'non-dual' in the sense of being inseparable. Metaphysically the term 'non-duality' is a 'contradiction in terms' – for it is impossible to conceive of any one thing without implying some actual or possible other. Non-duality is not a bland lack of distinction but a dynamic relation of inseparable distinction between any one thing, its larger field or context of appearance and everything else within that field.

16. **The triadic or 'Trika' school of tantric metaphysics is not reducible to a form of non-dualism or 'A-dvaita'.** That is because the principle of non-duality itself implicitly rests on a dualism or dichotomy of 'duality' and 'non-duality'. Just as any boundary both absolutely distinguishes the areas it bounds and at the same time makes them 'one' or inseparable, so is the general principle of *inseparable distinction* the essential principle and 'third term' ('Dvait-advaita') uniting 'duality' ('Dvaita') and 'non-duality' ('A-dvaita') in a true threefold, trinity or triad ('Trika'). In the Trika metaphysics of The Awareness Principle, the 'third term' of a triad is not the 'lowest' in a triple hierarchy but rather the most primordial - as 'Shiva-Shakti' is more primordial than either 'Shiva' or 'Shakti'.

17. **The aim and meaning of 'Yoga' is not just unity or *identification* of individual consciousness with the divine awareness, but the fullest**

224

individuation **of that awareness.** 'Being awareness' ('Chaitanayatma') is impossible without fully and completely being ourselves – individualising and embodying that awareness. The movement of spiritual development is two-way - not simply the individual soul or Jiva becoming Shiva but Shiva becoming more fully manifest as the individual soul or Jiva. It is only through identification with the divine awareness that the inexhaustible dimensions of our individuality, actual and potential, human and trans-human, can be freely and creatively explored, experienced and embodied, not just in physical life but in the multi-dimensional universe of pure awareness ('Shuddha Advha') of which our planet is but one limited, physical plane.

18. **Ego-identity is not identical with *individuality*, nor is the individual soul ('Jiva') a 'contraction' or 'limitation' of the universal or divine soul ('Shiva').** Only ego-identity and ego-awareness is limited and contracted, and yet this very contraction is nothing but the contracted and limiting awareness of our true *individuality* - one which prevents us from recognising the individual nature and potentials of our experienced self as a unique expression and embodiment of the divine awareness which is the experiencing self.

19. **'Yoga' as 'union' with the divine is not a bland merger, but an experienced *relation* with two distinct but inseparable aspects.** Thus we can utter and experience the mantram 'I am Shiva' ('Shivoham') with two quite distinct intonations. When we can say with truth that 'I am Shiva' we are speaking *as* Shiva. The 'I' in this intonation is the very 'I' *of* Shiva - expressing a state of transcendence of our limited, individual 'I'. When, on the other hand, we utter the mantram in the form 'I am Shiva', then we are speaking as and for ourselves, affirming that even our apparently limited self or 'I' *is* Shiva – is God - in individualised form. In this way we affirm or evoke an experience of the divine nature of our most individual self or 'I'. These two distinct intonations of the singular mantram 'Shivoham' ('Shiva am I') are inseparable. One is an experience of our 'I' as identical with that state of unbounded awareness bliss that is Shivatattva or Shivattva. The other is its converse – experiencing our self or 'I', in whatever state of being

and whatever the boundaries of our awareness, as an expression of Shiva. Together these two sides of the single mantram 'Shivoham' constitute twin poles of a singular dialectical and rhythmical relation that is the essence of 'union' with the divine - a meditational movement from one intonation and experience of the mantram to the other and back again. It is the dynamic relation of these poles that is their 'unity' - and the essence of yoga as 'union'.

20. **Liberation ('Moksha') as release from 'karma' and rebirth is not an ultimate end-stage of spiritual evolution but rather its true beginning.** Like death itself, liberation is a door, which allows us to leave the karmic 'nursery school' of human existences and begin to explore the multidimensional universe of awareness beyond it. Liberation then, is not an end but the beginning of an eternal and infinite new adventure in consciousness. Neither death nor liberation removes us from the realm of differentiated experiencing and reality as such. Instead identification with pure, undifferentiated awareness is what opens us to the multidimensional universe of awareness and to its countless, non-physical, but no less differentiated worlds of experiencing.

21. **It is the 'supreme' or 'great' self ('Paratma'/'Mahatma') of the individual and *not* any incarnate soul ('Sakala') that 'reincarnates' or has multiple incarnations.** No incarnate soul, self or person is the 'reincarnation' of another. Death is not simply a passage to re-birth but a return of the incarnate self to the soul world and to the soul womb of its 'great self' ('Mahatma'), that self whose awareness or 'soul' transcends and embraces countless different identities and incarnations - past, present and future, actual and possible. Birth is not a '*re*-incarnation' of a past identity or personality but a fresh and *new* incarnation and embodiment of our supreme soul ('Paratma') or great soul ('Mahatma').

22. **Life is not suffering and liberation from suffering and the cycle of rebirth is not the sole meaning of human existence.** To identify human life with 'suffering' is to deny all meaning to the unique living expression of the divine that is human creativity - thus invalidating the entire creative

journey of the individual human being and of human consciousness, culture and civilisation as a whole - past, present and future, along with the pleasure, learning and fulfilment that are its fruit. Those spiritual teachers who teach only freedom *from* do not know the true meaning of freedom as freedom *to*. They themselves are not truly free – for their own freedom 'to' is used solely in pursuit of ever-greater freedom 'from'. True freedom *to* is the 'power of the new'. It is the infinite, and free creative power ('Kriya-Shakti') of the divine awareness with which each creature, as an expression of it, is itself innately endowed, and through which all things are forever and freely manifested anew in each moment.

23. **The aim of identification with pure awareness is not transcendence of all so-called 'negative' emotions such as anger or grief.** On the contrary *identification with pure awareness* is what allows us to fully feel and affirm emotions of all sorts instead of losing ourselves in *unaware* identification with them and unaware expressions of them. Awareness, in other words, is not just freedom *from* emotions we have become identified with or attached to. It is also a freedom *to* – the freedom to feel those emotions even more fully but *without* losing ourselves in them. We cannot exercise this total *freedom to feel* without a pure awareness of our feelings that is by nature distinct from those feelings - and in this sense free *from* them. And yet the basic freedom bestowed by this freedom *from* is essentially a freedom *to*. Exercising this freedom to fully feel a so-called 'negative' emotion such as anger is *not* the same however, as 'getting angry'. 'Getting' angry or upset is a way of 'acting out' or 'evacuating' an emotion through our behaviour. Impulsively acting 'out' or reacting from our emotions is no less a *negation* of those emotions than repressing them - both are born of the fear of fully feeling them from within. That is why no true *guru* will express emotions in an unaware or purely reactive way - but neither will they presume or preach transcendence of any emotion.

24. **There are no such things as 'negative' feelings, only feelings we negate – refuse or fear to fully feel.** Yet living is feeling, and choosing to live means *choosing to feel*. We cannot feel fully alive without being fully alive to – fully aware of - our feelings. All of them. Indeed the most basic

capacity, power or 'Shakti' of pure awareness ('Shiva') is the capacity or power *to feel*. For awareness as such has an essentially *feeling* character – being that which allows us to know things and beings in a direct feeling way - rather than turning them into mere objects of mental or perceptual cognition. Total transcendence of feelings is not liberation but spiritual death. To be truly aware then, means being beware of self-styled 'Buddhists' who teach the use of the mind (Buddhi) to achieve freedom from emotions such as anger, for they are teachers not of life and spiritual liberation but of spiritual emptiness and death. And no spiritually exalted feeling or feelings – 'compassion' for example – can be affirmed and embodied if other feelings such as anger are negated. For as Abhinavagupta wrote: "Even the states of anger etc. exist because of their identity with the wondrous play of the divine consciousness, otherwise their very existence would be impossible … These states of anger etc., at the time of their arising are of the form of *nirvikalpa* i.e. they are the pure power of the divine … When their real nature is known, then these very states … bring about liberation in this life." Liberation brings with it a divine spiritual elevation, refinement, enrichment, and intensification of our feeling life, not its death or transcendence. Tantrism is about feeling all manner of feelings in the most directly sensual way, with and within our bodies. Hinduism in all its forms is imbued with great richness of feeling. Its major exported form however – Buddhism - offers spiritual 'peace' through emotional emptiness, and falsely pretends that compassion can be truly felt and expressed at the expense of other feelings such as anger.

25. **Pleasure is not a 'transient' part of life.** Indeed such beliefs were and remain the chief religious curse from which 'tantra' offers release and liberation – with its affirmation of sensual bliss and pleasure, of music, drama and arts, and the entire world of 'manifestation'. Thus the ever renewed and ever-new pleasure that can be derived from a single poem, painting or piece of music is inexhaustible and stays with us forever – it is not in any way transient. The same applies to both the sensual bliss of pure awareness and to the 'simple pleasures' of life, whether looking at a flower, enjoying sex, going for a walk or meeting a friend.

26. **'Pure' or 'transcendental' awareness' is not a 'supra-sensuous' awareness lacking all sensual qualities or differentiation.** Instead it has its own innately sensual qualities. Why else would the tantras speak in such sensual terms of the 'light' of awareness ('Prakasha'), its spatiality ('Akasha'), its all-pervasive air ('Prana') or its all-permeating bliss ('Ananda')? These terms are no mere metaphors but express direct experiences of the innate 'sensual-transcendental' qualities or divine 'soul qualities'. Through intensified awareness of ordinary sensory qualities such as colour, sound, shape, weight, brightness, warmth, density etc. we can come to experience the sensual qualities *of* awareness or soul which they manifest. Sensual qualities of pure awareness are essentially tonal qualities – sensed in the same way as the brightness or darkness, warmth or coolness, lightness or heaviness, shape, colour and texture of vocal or musical tones. Thus by attuning to the unique 'tone' of a particular colour or the unique 'colour' of a particular tone we can come to feel the pure soul tones and soul colours – inaudible and invisible to our outer senses - that lie behind them, and that give our souls their own innate bodily shape and tone.

27. **'Bodyhood', as 'boundedness', does not imply bondage, duality or separation.** A boundary both distinguishes and unites. Thus our body surface is a boundary, yet as a porous, sensing, breathing surface, it does not separate but both distinguishes and unites us with the space and air around us. Similarly, whilst a circle seems to bound an area of space within it, the circular or spherical boundary is not itself anything bounded – for it is precisely that which unites its inner space with the space around it. Like circles drawn on an infinite and unbounded sheet of paper, the boundaries of awareness that constitute the bodyhood of individual beings or consciousnesses do not simply delimit, contain, circumscribe their awareness or separate them from other beings or souls - for these boundaries, like circles or spheres are also what unite each soul with the *unbounded* space of awareness around them - and thus also with every other 'bounded' soul within that space. Were we able to BE the circle we draw on a blank page we would not experience it as a boundary or as bounding – nor would we experience any separation of 'inner' or 'outer'. It is by stretching ourselves to

and *becoming* the boundaries of our awareness that we automatically transcend those boundaries and all sense of boundedness.

28. **There is no such thing as a 'disembodied soul'.** Though soul (awareness) is not itself anything bodily or material, it is that which *bodies* and that which *matters* – giving rise to its own infinite, ever-changing bodily shapes or forms, both material and immaterial, physical and non-physical. The entire physical universe of matter is the body of the divine awareness or soul. Our own physical body is but a materialised body image of our soul and its eternal body – our divine awareness body ('Divyadeha'/'Vijnanadeha'). A so-called 'discarnate' soul in the afterlife is no longer a soul in physical form with a physical body – and yet is no less embodied in its own way.

29. **There is no such thing as an 'insentient' object, being or thing.** Since all things are manifestations of the divine awareness they are each endowed with awareness and thus also with sentience. The idea of 'insentience' is in contradiction to the truth that the divine awareness is present or immanent within all things. 'Things' are not simply insentient 'projections' or 'reflections' of the divine light of awareness but uniquely patterned expressions of it, radiating it forth from within. All 'objective' perception of things has an innately inter-subjective character. What we perceive as mere 'insentient' things are simply the outward perceptual form taken within our own humanly patterned field of awareness by the perceptual patterns of other non-human consciousnesses or subjectivities.

30. **The Awareness Principle is not simply a religious philosophy and practice aimed solely at liberating the individual soul from the limitations of ego-awareness and ego-identity.** Instead it emphasises the subversive social and scientific significance of The Awareness Principle in turning upside-down (or right-side up) the global world-view of Western science and the socio-economic culture it has created. For this is a world-view which insists on identifying basic reality with a universe of 'objects' and identifies truth itself with 'objectivity' rather than *Absolute Subjectivity* – that awareness that is the *a priori* condition or 'field condition' for our consciousness of any object, thing, being, self, world or universe whatsoever.

31. **Plurality and the infinite differentiation of the manifest universe of experience are not identical with ignorance ('Avidya') or an unreal delusion (Maya) veiling the ultimate reality of Absolute Subjectivity.** This was already recognised by Abhinavagupta when he argued "… if Brahman is accepted as having ignorance ('Avidya') as another beginningless element along with him, this [Vedantic] doctrine cannot be accepted as monistic."

32. **The 'monistic' principle of Advaita and Kashmir Shaivism is not one that abolishes all difference, but embraces all differentiated experiencing.** Only The Awareness Principle - the principle of *inseparable distinction* between awareness *as such* on the one hand, and anything we are aware *of*, on the other - explains how this can be, and why monism and pluralism, like monotheism and polytheism are not opposites. For differentiation does not imply separation but can be understood instead as an ever-changing *field* of elements, each and all of which are both distinct (and therefore plural) and inseparable or 'one'.

33. **The Awareness Principle is not a form of exclusivistic religious monotheism exalting a particular *being* as a supreme or sole divinity, but a divine-metaphysical monism** - one which recognises all divinities and all beings as *self-differentiations* of the divine absolute ('Anuttara'). The monism of The Awareness Principle is also a trinitarian, triadic or 'triune' monism - recognising the Divine Absolute in its three distinct aspects of awareness ('Shiva'), power of manifestation ('Shakti') and their inseparability ('Shiva-Shakti'). The Divine Absolute as such is the hidden and implicit 'fourth' ('Turya') of this triad – one that can be symbolised as a dot ('Bindu') at the centre of a triangle. The Metaphysics of Awareness is not only a triune monism but also a triune "monadology" - understanding all beings as irreducible units or 'monads' ('Anu') each of which is a distinct but inseparable differentiation of the Divine Absolute ('Anuttara'), and each of which unites its three distinct but inseparable aspects.

34. **The highest spiritual value affirmed through The Awareness Principle as in the Vedas is not a god or gods but Truth.** That is why all the

'Hindu' gods - including those worshipped in pre-Vedic, non-Vedic or trans-Vedic traditions such as tantra - are ultimately understood as diverse *personifications* of the truth of the Divine Awareness in its different aspects, and not seen as identical with it. The theology of The Awareness Principle is 'Hindu' in so far as what is known as 'Hinduism' - an umbrella term embracing countless convergent and divergent streams and schools of thought - is unique in being the one world religion which does not lay claim to the whole or sole truth, but instead recognises no religion, god or gender - as higher than Truth itself. The Truth of the Divine is recognised in The Awareness Principle - as in the Shaivist tantric teachings - not only in the form of the divine masculine (Shiva) or divine feminine (Shakti) but also as an androgyne and trans-gendered godhead 'Anuttara'. Nevertheless Shiva - that 'male' god which identifies the *primordial masculine* with *pure awareness* - is of greater significance today than ever before. This is because we no longer live in an old-fashioned patriarchal world but one increasingly imbalanced towards a distorted form of the feminine principle of action and expression. This finds expression in a global culture of materialism and violence, narcissism and media exhibitionism - and is still countered only by the masculine principle in the old, distorted and redundant form of repressive state and religious 'control'. Issues of gender and power are historically long bound up with conflict and contradiction. And yet: "THERE ARE NO CONTRADICTIONS EXCEPT THOSE WE NEED! Need to secure our private ego-domain by the very (demi) god-like judgements of acts of cutting dictions or decrees in the first place: releasing dictions, contradictions dissolve, and the infinitely rich singular multidimensional universe of grace and light appears as it already is. Indeed: 'Let go – let God', it really is as simple as that." (Michael Kosok)

35. **Liberation ('Moksha') is not a letting go or surrender of self to the Divine, or its dissolution within it.** Instead it is simply and purely a surrender of 'self-possession' – the sense of 'possessing' or 'owning' a self. Awareness cannot - in principle - be reduced to the private property of any self we are aware *of* or think of as 'ours'. That is why even the 'liberated', 'aware', 'experiencing' or 'knowing' self is no self we can be aware *of* - nor any self that 'has' or 'possesses' awareness. It can only be that self which *is*

awareness - singular and divine. Liberation means disowning and restoring *ownership* of our sense of self to God - that Divine Awareness from which alone all the elements of our self-experience arise. Limiting ego-awareness and ego-identity on the other hand, is nothing but the obscuring delusion that comes from identifying with the elements of our experiences and taking them as our 'own' – as 'me' or 'mine'. Believing itself to 'possess' a self or identity the ego lives in constant fear of losing its 'self-possession' or being 'possessed'.

36. **Overcoming the basic 'impurity' or limitation of ego-awareness ('Anavamala') does not mean ceasing to experience a differentiated world or individualised self.** It is only by taking the different elements of our experience as 'me' or 'mine' that we cease to experience the *Divine* - forgetting that they are but the Divine experiencing itself through, in and as us. 'Liberation' then, means being aware of all the elements of our experienced 'self' as a self-manifestation and self-experience of the Divine Awareness itself. This is an Awareness that is not 'mine' or 'yours' - yet which experiences itself *as* 'me' and 'you', 'him' and 'her', 'them' and 'us'. As such, it is truly Divine, for though not being 'yours' or 'mine', it is the source of all that 'I', you or anyone can experience as 'their' self and 'their' experience.

THE ULTIMATE METAPHYSICS
OF AWARENESS

The Primary Triad of Realms

Awareness (*Chit*) is the One sole and singular reality, that ultimate reality denoted in the *tantras* by the term *Anuttara* - meaning that 'un-surpassable' or 'non-higher' – and symbolised by *Paramashiva* (the 'Supreme' Shiva). In the triadic or 'Trika' metaphysics of The Awareness Principle, the One singular and divine Awareness embraces a primary triad (*Paratrika*) consisting of three distinct but inseparable ontological 'realms' or 'domains of reality':

1. *The realm of 'non-being' understood as pure creative Potentiality.* This is a non-extensional and non-physical *time-space* of awareness containing infinite potentialities of awareness - all the infinite potential shapes, patterns and qualities of awareness that can manifest as actually experienced things and beings, worlds and phenomena. It is the all-embracing womb of creation - including all possible *and* actual universes. It is symbolised tantrically by the supreme mother goddess (*Paramshakti* or *Kali*) and the *Kalachakra* or wheel of time.

2. *The realm of Actuality, creation or 'being'* - manifest physically as the entirety of extensional space-time and as all actually existing worlds and phenomena, both physical and trans-physical. This is the realm we normally identify with 'reality' as such, ignoring the fact that potentialities have as much reality as actualities. The realm of Actuality is symbolised by *Mayashakti* and the concept of *Prakriti* ('nature' or 'creation' as that which is called forth into being) as opposed to *Purusha* (pure awareness).

3. *The realm of creative actualisation or 'becoming'.* This is the 'in-between' realm or reality which is the very process of realisation as such – the process of constant creation by which potentialities are constantly and continuously actualising or realising themselves, constantly 'coming-to-be' or 'be-coming'. They do so through infinite, infinitesimal 'points of power' which pervade space and are comparable to black-white holes. This realm is symbolised tantrically as countless *Shaktis*, as it is by the *Bindu* (dot) and by the idea of 'zero-point energy' in physics.

Being as Be-ing

The unity of all three realms lies not only in the fact that they are fundamentally realms of awareness but in the essence of the *third realm* in particular. For though I have termed this the realm of 'Becoming', philosophy has traditionally opposed the concept of 'Being' - understood as static, unchanging presence - with that of 'Becoming', understood as constant flux or *change*. Yet what if the essence of *both* Being and Becoming is neither the simple, unchanging *presence* of things in awareness, nor their constant change, but rather their continuous *presencing* - their 'Be-ing'? What if, indeed, there 'is' *no-thing* 'out there' or 'in here' that is simply present, waiting to be perceived? What if, instead of there simply 'being' things of any sort that we then happen to be aware *of* there is ultimately nothing but awareness as such constantly and continuously *thinging* itself? No trees, branches, leaves, flowers or fruit but a constant treeing, branching, leafing, flowering and fruiting. No everyday objects like tables and chairs but the constant and sustained tabling and chairing of each table or chair. What if there is no matter but a constant mattering or 'materialising' of awareness – not my awareness or yours but the One, universal or Ultimate Awareness? What if not only things but their sensory qualities are not simply *present*, but constantly and continuously *presencing*? What if we were able to experience a colour such as orange, for example, as a constant *orange-ing*, a shape such as roundness as a constant *round-ing*, and a material texture such as wood as a constant *wood-ing*?

The understanding of 'Becoming' not simply as change or transformation but as 'coming-to-be' or 'be-coming' – as 'Be-ing', is central. For true *wonder* at the fact that anything *is* at all is impossible unless we are able to directly experience their 'Being' or 'is-ness' in a wholly new way - not as some sort of one-off creation out of Nothingness - *ex nihilo* - that leaves them simply 'there', present to our awareness and either changing or not-changing, but rather as their constant emergence or *presencing* from and within awareness – their Be-ing. The Being of things understood as simple co-presence in awareness is the essence of space. Understood as their Be-ing on the other hand – their continuous *presencing* - it is the essence of time. The world around us and everything in it is indeed in this sense, not simply 'there' at all. There is indeed 'no-thing' that simply 'is' in the sense of being present. Yet the terror of Non-Being or 'Nothingness' in *this* sense – of 'no-thing-ness' – can at once be removed by sheer wonder and gratefulness for the constant *thinging* of things, their Be-ing. 'Being' is usually thought of as a state. Rethinking it as 'Be-ing' however, Being is not a state but a process. It is 'no-thing' and yet neither is it Nothing. Instead it is a continuous process of creative actualisation or Action. What unites all *three* realms of awareness therefore is not only Awareness as such (Shiva) and its innate potentials, but also the actualisation or presencing of these potentials through the innate 'power of action' which is the essential meaning of 'Shakti'. Shiva and Shakti. Awareness of Potentiality and its perpetual presencing or actualisation, are inseparable aspects of the divine. Thus *we* do not need to 'actualise' our being or 'self'. For it is constantly *being* actualised, constantly presencing in awareness. This is the meaning of Being as 'Be-ing'.

The Realms of Possibility and Parallelity

Just as the same inspiration, source or mood could give rise, in a human being, to a painting or piece of music, and just as a stem cell can give rise to a host of specific cell types, so can creative Potentialities always find more than one *possible* form of actualisation. Furthermore however, the realm of Potentiality is itself constantly being enriched by *new* Possibilities. For just as one thought or thing automatically implies or gives rise to another, so does all creative Action automatically imply and give rise to multiple *further* Possibilities of Action - of actualisation or manifestation. Thus there is also an endless cyclical or rather spiral relation uniting the 3rd realm (that of creative Action or Actualisation) with the 1st realm (that of creative Potentiality) through the 2nd realm (that of all that is constantly being Actualised). In addition to the triad of the three primary realms (Potentiality or Non-Being, Actuality or Being, and Actualisation as 'Be-ing') we must recognise a fourth – the realm of Possibility. All Action and Actualities then, emerge not simply from the 1st realm of pure Potentiality therefore, but from a Realm of Possible actions and actualities - one that is both latent in the realm of Potentiality and at the same time constantly being expanded through the very *process* of Actualisation. Yet the question then arises – what 'becomes' of the 'Alternate' Possibilities *generated* by the process of Actualisation in any given domain or world of Actuality but not themselves actualised *within* it? The answer is that these not only feed back into the 1st realm, that of pure Potentiality - but also find expression in a realm of Alternate or Parallel Actualities. This is what I term the realm of Alternity or Parallelity - recognised in quantum physics through the Parallel Worlds theory of Hugh Everett.

The result of these considerations is that in addition to the triad of three primary domains of reality so far considered – those of Potentiality, Actuality and the process of Actualisation – the action of *realisation* as such - we must add three further realms: a realm of constantly multiplying Possibilities of Action *without* which no *free* action or choice would be possible and *within* which all actions and choices first occur, a realm of Parallel actualities in which *alternate* Possibilities are chosen and actualised. These are in turn united by a realm of Reciprocal Action - whereby Possibilities actualised in one world or actuality both spring from and generate un-Actualised possibilities in another Alternate or Parallel world. For whilst in any one 'Actual' reality the Parallel realities in which Alternate Possibilities of action are Actualised appear as mere *imaginary possibilities* - in those Alternate or Parallel realities themselves, these Possibilities are experienced as *fully real* – as Actualities. Our every experience and action then, is not just the Actualisation of a Potentiality within the Actuality of our own world (the one we take as sole reality) but also the Actualisation - from within a vast realm of Possible actions - of alternate actions and experiences within Alternate Actualities or 'Parallel Worlds'.

This principle applies to the 'self' or 'I' also. For that self or 'I' which does or experiences one thing in one world or sphere of Actuality is 'itself' not the *same* self or 'I' as that which experiences or enacts another Possibility in a parallel but Alternate Actuality. Together then, with 'Parallel' or 'Alternate' Actions and Actualities, worlds and universes, go Parallel and Alternate selves. These multiple selves, actions, possibilities and actualities are united only by a higher Awareness - one which embraces not only the three primary realms of Potentiality, Actuality and Action or Actualisation, but also the three, no less significant realms of Possibility, Alternate or Parallel Actualities - and their Reciprocity. Pure Awareness *alone* is the primordial 'zero-realm' that embraces all the other six realms or domains of reality.

The Six Fundamental Realms of Awareness

1. *The Realm or Reality of Potentiality* that is the source of all.

2. *The Realm of Actuality* that we normally identify with reality *per se*.

3. *The Realm of Actualisation or Action* as such - of reality as *realisation*.

4. *The Realm of Possibility* – of multiple possible actions and actualities.

5. *The Realm of Alternity or Parallelity* – of Parallel but Alternate Actualities.

6. *The Realm of Reciprocity* – the reciprocal relation of Actual and Alternate realities.

The Seventh Realm – Plurality

The realm of Parallelity embraces not just countless alternate or parallel *physical* realities, but also an infinite Plurality of *pre-physical* and *trans-physical* realms, domains, or 'planes' of awareness. In each of these planes (Sanskrit *Loka*) *experiencing* takes on a wholly different nature and wholly different forms to those we are used to in the physical plane – as it does in the plane of dreaming awareness for example. In all of these trans-physical realms, the experienced *relation* between the six *fundamental* realms of awareness is different in one way or another. In the domain of dreaming awareness for example, as in the first trans-physical plane we enter in the life-between-lives, Actualities are less fixed and we experience with far more immediacy that constant process of Actualisation or 'Be-ing' whereby different elements of our experience, inner and outer, are both constantly coming-to-be or arising and also passing away - as in a dream. The realms of dreaming and of the after-life are experienced directly as realms of 'Becoming' in the traditional sense – of arising *and* passing away. In yet other realms of the life-between lives we have the opportunity to experience Parallel realities simultaneously, and to explore, in pseudo-physical form, all the Alternate lives we might have led on earth. The 1ˢᵗ primary realm of awareness – the realm of Potentiality – is an intensional 'time-space' of awareness circumscribing space-time itself, and embracing all Potential, Possible and all Parallel Actualities – including what we perceive physically as 'past', 'present' and 'future' existences and Actualities. This 'time-space' is not one-dimensional – an experience of one thing following another in a single line of 'space-time'. Instead it is an *awareness* that spans and embraces multiple moments in time and multiple lifetimes simultaneously. From its perspective, all lifetimes are simultaneous or co-present, and there is no moment of any of our lives that is not constantly and eternally *being* lived. Moments do not simply constitute a 'present' which then disappear into the Past to be superseded by 'Future' moments. Instead all that is experienced as 'present' is constantly *presencing* – constantly emerging from the realm of Possibility and constantly giving rise to Alternate 'past' and 'future' Actualities.

So-called 'reincarnational' existences on the physical plane are but one linear, temporal dimension of the realm of Alternity or Parallelity. This realm also embraces countless *non-physical* as well as physical planes of reality, all of which together constitute the realm of Plurality - a multi-dimensional universe or multi-verse of awareness, made up of countless planes of awareness. These are all 'Parallel' planes in the sense that each is defined by one of an infinite number of Alternate Possible modes of experiencing. Thus what may be perceived as variations of material 'mass', 'density' or form on the physical plane may be experienced as variations of light, of colour or of quasi-musical 'tone' of feeling in different non-physical planes – and vice versa. What is experienced as 'inner' on one plane may be experienced as 'outer' in another – or as neither inner nor outer. In general, what is experienced within the 'higher' non-physical planes takes the form of psychical 'qualia' – sensed and sensual qualities of awareness as such. Instead of perceiving 'space' as a physical expanse before our eyes for example, it will be experienced as a spacious field or expansion of awareness as such. Whereas on the physical plane a feeling of warmth or coolness towards another person might express itself as physical closeness or distance to them, on non-physical planes, what we ordinarily experience as spatial closeness and distance (or as physical warmth or coolness) is experienced purely as warmth or coolness of *feeling*. Phenomena such as light, warmth, colour and sound are experienced on non-physical planes not as *sensory qualities of objects*, but rather as *sensual qualities of awareness* – light being experienced as luminous radiance of awareness itself, and colours and tones as felt colourations or tones of awareness – comparable to what we sense as tones or colourations of *mood*.

From Metaphysics to Physics

Physics used to be identified with a mechanistic view of the universe in which everything consisted of *matter in motion*. Quantum physics has effectively made the notion of solid matter meaningless. For on an ultra-microscopic or quantum level, such 'things' as mass, momentum, energy, space and time, cease to be separately quantifiable or even definable realities - even 'particles' such as electrons turning out to have the same non-localised *wave* character as light. In dispelling 'the myth of matter' quantum physics has also made redundant our common but mythical idea of *motion*. When we view objects and people moving on a TV screen we know at the back of our minds that we are not actually observing 'matter in motion' but simply multiple points of light with different colours or 'wavelengths' turning on and off at different fixed points on the screen – and in doing so forming regular patterns on that screen which

244

appear like familiar material objects and seem to be in motion. From a quantum-physical perspective however, *all* perceived motion, even motion in what we perceive as three-dimensional space, has the same character as motion on a flat two-dimensional screen. Nothing – 'no-thing' *actually* moves 'in' space. There is simply a potential for seeing things at varying points in space. When a ball has been thrown it is no more than a visual image of motion in space of the sort created by points of light on a flat screen. Yet as Samuel Avery convincingly argues, behind our *visual* image of the ball in motion lurks a potential *tactile* sensation – that of catching and feeling the ball in our hands. It is this potential for tactile sensation that makes us sense the ball not just as a visual 'image' we can see but as 'solid' matter. Similarly, it is because we are *aware* that the food we actually *see* on our TV dinner plate can also *potentially* be touched and tasted that we regard it as having more 'materiality' than a mere photograph or TV image of food on a plate. The TV image itself only seems to be 'real' – matter like - in so far as it reminds us of these potential qualities – we can also recall or imagine the tactile sensation of feeling a ball or the taste sensation of eating a meal that we see on TV. In Avery's words: "It is the potential for tactile sensation that makes a visual image 'physical'." And more generally "The concept of material substance … is derived from *potential* perceptions in each sensory realm." [my stress].

In other words, what we think of as 'matter' is nothing simply actual but rather a *relation* between actual experiences in *one* sensory dimension of experience (for example the visual) and *potential* experiences in another (for example the tactile dimension). For not only do all actual experiences begin as potential experiences – as potential patterns or qualities of awareness. They also seem all the *more* 'actual' to the extent that, like the experience of seeing a ball coming towards us, they are accompanied by an awareness of *potential* experiences such as moving to catch the ball and feeling it in our hands. Yet even the apparent motion of our own bodies in catching a ball is not an example of 'matter' in motion. There is no motion of our body 'in' space – merely the awareness of subjective *sensations* of motion, and of different actions such as catching a ball. The essence of all bodily 'action' then, is not 'actually' any sort of objective motion of our bodies in space but rather the *actualisation* of *potential patterns of sensation*. Both 'matter' and its 'motion' then, are nothing essentially objective but rather an *awareness* of *potential* dimensions and patterns of sensory experiencing within actual ones. Matter is therefore 'real' only in the root sense of the word as 'mother' [mater] of all things - being the maternal womb or matrix of potentiality – more specifically a realm of *potential patterns and qualities* of *awareness*. These then find experience as *actual* patterns and qualities of *sensory experiencing*.

The 'metaphysical' realm of Potentiality then, can be said to consist of countless potential *field-patterns and field-qualities* of awareness – comparable to the countless potential images that a flat two-dimensional screen could display. The realm of 'physical' Actuality on the other hand, consists of actually *patterned fields and qualities* of awareness – comparable to all the images we actually perceive, not just on two-dimensional screens, but as the overall four-dimensional field of sensory awareness that we experience as the physical world. The realm of Plurality is comparable to the countless actual channels or web images available to us for viewing on a TV or computer screen. The Realm of Alternity or Parellelity can be compared to all the *alternate* TV channels, web-pages and video streams that are constantly and concurrently running in parallel within the realm of Plurality – 'unreal' for those who may not be aware of them at all, but real for those who are aware of them and for whom they become actual by viewing them. The realm of Reciprocity can be compared to the way in *which alternate possible* TV channels, programmes and websites not only define themselves by the reciprocal relation but have a way of multiplying by simultaneously differentiating themselves from and mimicking one another. Indeed they may even mutually and reciprocally incorporate one another – as when one webpage or website offers links to another, one TV channel advertises or shows broadcasts bought from another - or even *displays* a broadcast running on another channel in an internal frame. Experiential phenomena are recognisably formed patterns or 'matrices' of sensory qualities, like patterned points of light on a screen. Yet the patterns and sensory qualities that give form to experienced phenomena as such do not themselves posses any actual and tangible sensory form. By this I mean that though we may experience a phenomena such as a 'heavy red ball' - seeing it, touching it, feeling it and picking it up - we cannot pick up our sense of its heaviness, or our perception of its roundness or redness. For redness and roundness *as such* exist only *as* ideas – in reality there being no pure or perfectly round objects and no way of perceiving 'redness' independently of a particular hue of red. Indeed the phenomenal form we perceive and think of as 'a ball' is not itself anything material or actual, for the very idea of 'ballness' is rooted in potential ways of actively relating to the phenomenon – of handling, throwing or kicking it for example.

Whereas the sensory experience of a phenomenal form is something physically tangible, the very patterns and qualities that constitute phenomenal forms, though we take them as objective are, are essentially 'all in the mind'. Forms are mental 'ideas' – which is why the Greek word *eidos* meant both 'idea' and 'form'. In the history of European thought it was Plato who first argued for the pure *ideality* of material forms, seeing experienced or 'phenomenal' forms as their shadow reflection. Plato understood pure Ideas or Forms as belonging to an immaterial and transcendent realm. Aristotle understood matter (Greek *hyle*) as potentiality, and form (*morphe*) as actuality. Actuality results from a capacity (*dynamis*) for formative activity (*energeia*) – a process of actualisation which leads towards the realisation of an ideal form or pattern (*entelecheia*) that is not transcendent but *immanent* in all things as their inner aim, purpose or direction of development (*telos*). Similarly, Thomas Aquinas, following Aristotle, understood 'primary matter' (*Prima Materia*) as nothing actual or substantial but rather as pure *potentiality* - a type of formless and 'passive potentiality' inseparable from God as 'active potentiality', the potentiality for the emergence of actual form and for change of form or transformation. These Aristotelian understandings of 'matter' are reflected today in Rupert Sheldrake's notion of biological forms and transformations as a result of 'morphogenesis' - the progressive actualisation of non-physical patterns or 'morphic fields'.

The accusation levelled against the 'God-concept' of religion – namely that God cannot be actually seen, has no sensory qualities or definable location apply equally to the Matter-concept of science. Both the God-concept and the Matter-concept can be seen as substitutes or 'placeholders' for the recognition of that womb-like realm of Potentiality – that is no less *real* than anything we actually experience. Physical 'matter' is real only in the root sense of the word - being the divine 'mother' [*mater*] and 'mind' of all things - a womb of potentiality bearing within the mental patterns, idea-shapes or *matrices* of all possible actualities. This is not a new thought but one long recognised by philosophers, physicists and theologians alike.

'Matter' can be seen as the very 'mind' of God - understood as an *awareness* of every potential pattern or 'idea-shape' of things. This being the case, who should mind and why should it matter if we call the primordial awareness mind or matter, 'The Mind of God', The Great Mother, 'The Matrix' or the 'Prima Materia'? If you don't mind, it doesn't matter. Yet if 'It', this universal or divine 'mother', 'mind' or 'matrix' of all things, didn't quite literally 'matter' – materialising and actualising itself from a realm of pure potentiality -

there would literally *be* no thing that we could either experience or conceive of scientifically *as* physical 'matter'. What we experience as physical matter emerges or manifests from the realm of the Potential – this very process of 'emergence' (Greek *physis*) being the root meaning of the terms 'physics' and 'physical' themselves. Any 'meta-level' consideration of the nature of 'physics' is of course, by nature 'meta-physical' – transcending the bounds of physics as a science. Yet the latter, as we have seen, leads us right back to the multiple metaphysical realms of the Ultimate - understood as that ultimate awareness that in the *tantras* went by the name of *Anuttara*.

THE AWARENESS PRINCIPLE SUMMARISED

Definition

A new philosophical foundation for religion, science and everyday life.

Roots

The 'A-dvaita' or 'non-dual' school of Indian philosophy. In particular the schools of yoga and philosophical theology known collectively as 'Shaiva Advaita', 'Shaivist Tantrism' or 'Kashmir Shaivism'.

Basic Principle

Awareness as such and anything we are or could be aware of are like two sides of a coin, both inseparable and perfectly distinct.

Similarly the whole principle of 'monism', 'unity' or 'non-duality' implies neither separation nor loss of all distinction.

The true 'monistic' principle of 'non-duality' is inseparable distinction.

Space and Awareness 1

We are aware of things in space.

Those things cannot be separated from the empty space around or within them (atoms are largely space too).

Nevertheless that space remains absolutely distinct from anything and everything we are aware of in it.

Like 'empty' space, awareness as such – 'pure' awareness' - cannot be separated from particular, tangible things we are aware of.

Nevertheless it remains absolutely distinct from them.

Space and Awareness 2

If there were no such thing as space itself we could not be aware of anything within it. Space as such is therefore the pre-condition for us being aware of anything in it.

Similarly, awareness as such is the precondition for us being aware of anything at all, including space itself.

Ultimately, what we perceive as 'empty' space is nothing but the field of pure awareness necessary for us to be aware or 'conscious' of anything at all within it.

Space is essentially nothing 'physical' or 'objective'. Instead it is a dimension of awareness or subjectivity – one way of experiencing pure awareness.

'Awareness' and 'Consciousness' 1

Awareness and 'consciousness' are inseparable and yet fundamentally distinct.

If people 'lose themselves' through absorption in watching TV or a movie, reading a book or playing computer games, in work or domestic chores, in talking or making love, in sensations of pleasure or pain, or just in trains of thought or strong emotions, then they are still 'conscious' - but they are not fully aware.

'Awareness' and 'Consciousness' 2

Whenever our 'consciousness' becomes overly focussed on, fixated by, absorbed in or identified with any one thing, we lose awareness of our body and sensory environment as a whole, and all the other things and bodies within it.

In this sense, 'consciousness' is contracted awareness.

If, on the other hand, we can experience something or engage in some activity without losing a more expanded consciousness – one that can simultaneously embrace other things, thoughts, feelings and possible activities within it - then we are aware.

In this sense 'awareness' is expanded consciousness.

Awareness, Consciousness and Space

Awareness has the same nature as space. It always embraces countless things, and can never be fully absorbed in, or contained by or reduced to any one thing or set of things.

Like time, space is a dimension of awareness – understood as an expanded and ultimately unbounded spacious field of consciousness.

In this sense awareness is *field consciousness*.

Consciousness on the other hand, is the contraction of this field of awareness to a specific focus.

In this sense consciousness is *focal awareness*.

Locality and Non-Locality

We can locate an object 'in' space, but space as such, even though it can be divided and has many dimensions, has no location.

Similarly, awareness has an essentially non-local or field character.

Awareness fields are essentially non-local, whereas anything we are conscious of or aware of within them has a local or localisable character – whether an object in space, a feeling we experience in a part of our body, or a thought we are aware of in our head.

Loci and Foci of Awareness

Awareness is ultimately one singular, multidimensional field.

Every thing and every being in that field is a specific centre or 'locus' of awareness.

It is also a possible 'focus' of awareness for another such locus of awareness.

Each of us is a centre or locus of awareness able to focus our awareness on other such centres or loci of awareness – whether in the form of things or people.

As centres or loci of awareness, each of us is also but one centre or locus of a singular, multi-dimensional awareness field.

The One and the Many

The infinite, multidimensional awareness field is 'God' - the source of everything and every being.

Every thing and being is a unique field-pattern of awareness, one that in turn shapes its own uniquely patterned awareness field – its own uniquely perceived experiential world or environment.

The divine awareness field is therefore a field of fields – a holofield embracing the individual awareness fields of every thing and being.

We perceive all things according to our own field-patterns of awareness and from our own centres or loci of awareness.

Yet what we perceive is itself a unique field-pattern of awareness with its own uniquely patterned awareness field or experiential world.

Unity in Diversity

What unites all things and beings is that they are each centres of the infinite multi-dimensional world of awareness that is God, and that their own individual experienced worlds or awareness fields are but one part of that larger and divine 'field of fields' or 'Holofield'.

Each individual's awareness field is bounded only by the limitations and horizon of their own awareness.

The divine awareness field is unbounded and yet it both embraces and experiences itself through the individual awareness fields of each and every being, knowing itself as their common source and centre.

This common source and centre is God - understood as a divine "singularity of awareness" (Michael Kosok) uniting all individual centres of awareness as their essential or divine 'Self', and uniting also all the individual awareness fields that make up their experiential and perceptual Worlds.

Illustrations of Field and Focal Awareness

Diagram 1: 'Field Awareness' - elements of our experience (sensations or emotions, thoughts or things) experienced within and as a part of a spacious, non-localised field of awareness.

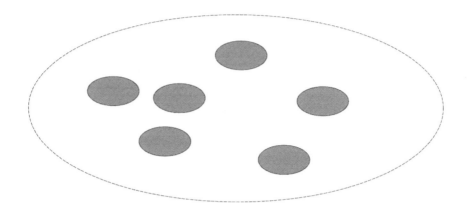

Diagram 2: 'Field attention' - attending to a specific element of our experience within and as a part of a spacious field of awareness i.e. attending from Field Awareness.

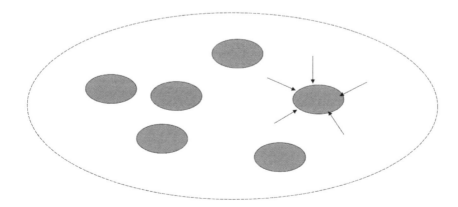

Diagram 3: 'Localised Awareness' – elements of the field experienced from the 'locus' of awareness constituted by one element within it (for example, looking at things or thoughts we are aware of solely 'through the lens' of one particular thought or from the perspective of one particular person). The result of identification with elements of our experience.

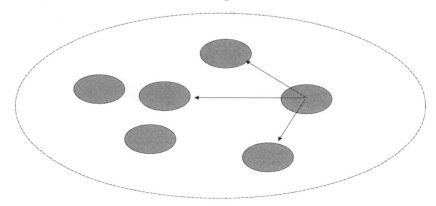

Diagram 4: 'Focalised Attention'. Elements of the field focussed on and objectified by one dominant element or complex of elements – 'the ego' - which does not experience either itself or its objects as parts of a field of awareness but sees those objects as separate and apart from one another, and experiences *itself* as a localised subject separate and apart from its objects.

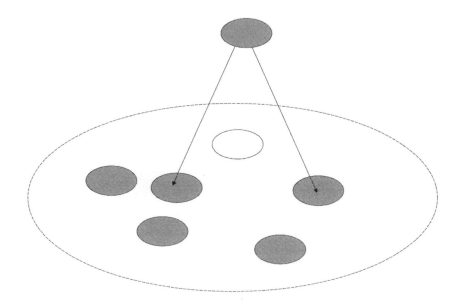

Diagram 5: 'Transcendental-Immanent Awareness' - the awareness field experiencing itself as not only embracing and transcending but immanent within and pervading all of its elements.

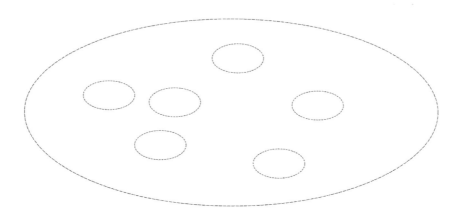

Diagram 6: Field Awareness as an awareness embracing both potential or emergent elements of experience (white ovoids) and actually present elements (grey ovoids).

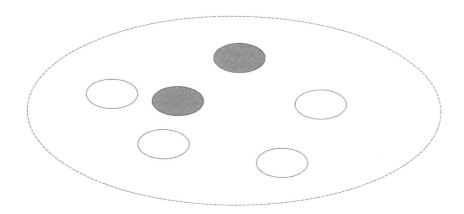

CONCLUDING VERSE

Awareness

Is no 'thing'.

Yet it is not 'nothing'.

It is that which first allows us to

Be aware of any 'Thing' whatsoever.

Not least our own body, and

That of all other

'Things'.

'Awareness' is no

Mere abstract, intellectual concept.

For what more basic and primordial dimension of

Any being's tangible, lived experience can there be,

If not the very awareness that they themselves *are*,

The primordial *awareness of being*,

And of the particularities of

Their own being?

If *the* most

Primordial experience

Of any being is *awareness* of Being

And of their own particularity as a being,

How then can awareness be a property of 'Being',

Let alone particular beings?

If awareness of our own bodies
And of a whole world of bodies in space and time
Is a no less primordial experience than awareness of
Being, then how can awareness as such be the
Property of *any* body - let alone a mere part
Of our own body - the brain?

Awareness is not simply something
Dwelling like a 'soul' within our bodies,
Let alone locked up in our heads and brains.
For in the same way that, as bodies, we dwell within space,
So also, as beings, do we dwell *within* awareness.
We ourselves are pervaded by awareness,
As our bodies are pervaded by space.

Awareness is no 'thing' we can find 'in' space,
Nor it is anything enclosed by our bodies or brains.
Instead awareness *is* the very space, inner and outer
Within which we experience all things.
To *be* awareness is to be the very
space, inner and outer, in which
We experience all things.

Awareness, like space,
Is that which first 'makes room'
For all things to *be* - to 'ex-ist' or 'stand out'
In space, and to *become*, in time,
All that they potentially *are*.

The very *being* of awareness

Is nothing else but *awareness* of being.

And yet awareness embraces more than being,

More than all beings, and more than everything that Is.

For Awareness includes awareness of 'non-being' too,

Which is not a void of 'nothingness', but a plenum or

Fullness of *potentiality* - transcending every

Actual thing or being, and yet immanent

Within all things and beings.

'Potential' realities, can

In principle, have reality

Only subjectively - within awareness.

They can therefore be nothing else but

Potentialities *of* awareness, its own limitless

Potentiality for differentiation and for

Individualisation in the form of

Actual things and beings.

Awareness

Bridges and spans

That most primordial abyss

Between non-being and being,

Potentiality and actuality,

Out of which all beings,

And all worlds

Arise.

As the pre-condition

For us being aware of any

Thing or any universe of things,

As the pre-condition too, for each and every theory

We might create about the things we are aware of,

Awareness - though 'no-thing - is, in principle

The sole possible and the sole thinkable

'Theory of Everything'.

Awareness is also the

Sole possible concept of 'God',

Not a Supreme Being 'with' awareness,

But that Supreme Awareness that

Is the source of all beings.

The recognition that Awareness is,

In principle, the ultimate reality or 1st Principle

Underlying and pervading all realities, is

'THE AWARENESS PRINCIPLE'.

About Peter Wilberg & 'The New Yoga of Awareness'

There are many who follow 'yogic' and 'tantric' practices derived from Indian religious traditions, just as there are teachers all over the world who seek to transmit the deeper wisdom of those traditions, and those who study and research these traditions as devoted scholars. Yet it is rare to find writings such as those of Peter Wilberg – which offer a new bridge between in-depth scholarly and philosophical study of such traditions on the one hand, and their exposition and practice in different contemporary schools of yoga and tantra on the other. Fewer still are teachers and authors who do not merely write 'on' or 'about' these traditions, but instead are able to offer a wholly original contribution *to* them, intuitively re-conceiving both their philosophy and practices – and doing so from new depths and breadths of awareness as well as deep study and broad learning. Peter Wilberg is one of these rare few. That is why, amidst the mountains of literature and thousands of courses and websites on 'Yoga' and 'Tantra', the teachings of Peter Wilberg on 'The New Yoga' do indeed have something fundamentally *new* to say, not least about the very meaning of such basic terms as 'Yoga' and 'Tantra', 'Vedanta' and 'Advaita', 'Meditation' and 'Mindfulness', 'Prana', 'Kundalini' etc. That is because his aim has always been not just to share his own embodied spiritual awareness or 'inner knowing' but to crystallise it into a comprehensive new *body of spiritual knowledge* - one relevant not just to the life of the individual, but to our whole understanding of society, the sciences, religion and the future of human civilisation.

'The New Yoga of Awareness' is a body of refined 'yogic' knowledge built on the foundation of 'The Awareness Principle' and 'The Practice of Awareness'. It offers a wealth of new spiritual-scientific insights to all types of readers, whether those familiar with traditional yogic and tantric practices or not, whether practitioners or teachers, scholars or philosophers, Hindus or Buddhists, Christians, Jews or Muslims. That is because Peter Wilberg, who understands himself as a "Tantric Hindu Gnostic Christian Socialist Jew", has reinterpreted the inner meaning of Eastern religious terminology, thought and practices in the broadest possible global and historical context. In particular however, he saw how his own unique inner experiences found their reflection in the different schools of Tantric religious philosophy known collectively as 'Kashmir Shaivism' or 'Shaivist Tantrism'. As a result, he has been able to reinterpret this highly refined spiritual tradition on a new experiential basis and within a wholly new conceptual and terminological framework, one which he calls simply 'The Awareness Principle'. 'The Awareness Principle' and 'The Practice of Awareness' constitute the two inseparable aspects of 'The New Yoga of Awareness'. The New Yoga then, is an entirely new range of practices or 'Yogas' of awareness founded on 'The Awareness Principle'. Together they offer not only simple but profound life-principles for the individual to practice, but also powerful new forms of Tantric pair- and partner meditation. These are rooted in an entirely new understanding of 'tantric sex' (Maithuna) as the expression of a spiritual but highly sensual intercourse of soul – as *soul body* intimacy and intercourse.

The Principles and Practices of Awareness which make up The New Yoga of Awareness unite religion, psychology and metaphysics in a way that truly makes it not just 'a' new yoga but THE New Yoga - effectively an entirely new and contemporary school of Tantra, and a rebirth of Tantric wisdom both *from* and *for* today's world. As such it has tremendous relevance *to* that world – not only scientifically and theologically but also for the psychological health of individuals, human relations and the world as a whole. That is because 'The Awareness Principle' provides a radically new philosophical foundation for our understanding not only of religion but of science and society – see www.thenewscience.org and www.thenewsocialism.org.

It is the purpose of Peter Wilberg's writings to make this new Tantric Wisdom known to the world in order that it can work *for* the world - reawakening in us all a recognition of that Divine Awareness which is the absolute or unsurpassable reality ('Anuttara') behind all realities. The nature of this Divine Awareness ('Shiva') and its immanent and autonomous creative power ('Shakti') was hitherto most clearly recognised in the Tantric religious philosophy of Kashmir Shaivism. Through The New Yoga however, the profound wisdom of this local and little-known historic tradition can now serve a much-needed contemporary global purpose – that of resisting 'The New Atheism' and the secular 'Monotheism of Money' that dominate today's world – along with the unquestioned assumptions of the purely technological 'Science' that is *its* new 'religion. In this way, The New Yoga can help bring an end to the rising ocean of spiritual ignorance, and to the grave ecological devastation, economic inequalities and global mayhem that go with it. The New Yoga is a way of accomplishing this world-transforming aim not through Jihad, violence or war, but through the supreme principle and innate power of Awareness. It makes known again that 'God' which is not simply one being among others 'with' awareness, but IS awareness – an unbounded awareness that is the divine source of all beings, yet also immanent within them all as their eternal and divine Self.

Biography

Acharya Peter Wilberg is an Indian spiritual teacher reborn in North-West London in 1952 of German and German-Jewish parentage. Peter Wilberg's past-life and inter-life spiritual knowledge, psychic abilities and profound intellect came to expression in his early childhood - during which he already cultivated and practiced advanced yogic powers or 'Siddhis'. When only eight years old he spontaneously wrote an essay for his Religious Education class which expressed the essence of the Hindu- Tantric philosophy of time (Kaala), creative vibration (Spanda), and 'energy' (Shakti). Whilst still in primary school he practiced the yoga of dreaming – the ability to visualise and enter a dream directly from the waking state with his dream body – and retain full awareness within the dream. He also used daily classical music listening to cultivate a yoga of 'inner sound' and 'feeling tone'. This involved using his face and eyes as an instrument by which to express, embody and amplify the inner music of the soul – its tonal qualities of feeling. Later he assiduously cultivated a new 'yoga of the face' with which, simply by meditating the 'inner sound' of their look and facial expression, he could directly sense the inner feeling tones or 'soul' of another person within his own body.

Acharya Peter Wilberg first practiced the yoga of 'out-of-body' travel as an adolescent. Yet in early adulthood, whilst studying philosophy at Oxford's Magdalen College, he was a frequent invisible flyer over its quads. Whilst studying philosophy Acharya Peter Wilberg gave deep attention to Eastern as well as Western thought. His subsequent MA dissertation in Humanistic Psychology was an expression of his experience of the yoga of dreaming – being based on experiential research into inter-personal dimensions of 'lucid dreaming'. In his own lucid dreams he encountered numerous teachers and Gurus, travelled beyond our planetary system and experienced planes of awareness beyond the dream state.

This phase of his work culminated in a single dream which led him beyond the dream state itself into a deeper layer of awareness and a profound trans-personal experience of his own 'great soul' or 'Mahatma'. .From within it he was wordlessly imbued with its higher knowing or 'Vijnana', as well as being and instructed with his spiritual life-mission – that of re-conceptualising that knowing in a new, more refined ways. Over subsequent decades he therefore continued to practice and seek new ways of articulating his many self-discovered Yogas, in particular that of using his face and eyes to mirror the looks of others and sense their souls - feeling their own soul in his body and his own soul in theirs. As a result, in 1975 he had the first experience of what was to become the new mode of 'Tantric Pair Meditation' that he describes in his essays and books – a form of tantric union or 'Maithuna' that he has now practiced for over 30 years. Through it, he cultivated his most important 'Siddhi' – the capacity, through his inner gaze and inner touch, to not only embody different qualities and faces of the Divine-Universal Awareness, but also to channel them directly into the body of another.

It was out of this rich history of continuous yogic practice and aware inner experiencing that Acharya Peter Wilberg was able to fulfil his life-mission and to formulate, over many decades, the original Principles and Practices of Awareness which make up 'The New Yoga'. In doing so, Peter Wilberg has not only become the preceptor or Acharya of a new spiritual teaching. He has also become an empowered and initiatory 'Guru' ('Siddha Guru' or 'Diksha Guru') in the most traditional sense – capable not only of embodying Divine potentials and powers of awareness ('Siddhis') but also awakening them in others – thus bestowing initiation ('Diksha').

Together with his lifelong studies of both Indian and European philosophies, this extraordinary experiential history enabled Acharya Peter Wilberg to evolve, over several decades, the metaphysical principles and meditational practices which together make up what he calls 'The New Yoga' – a yoga of pure awareness (Shiva) and its innate potentials and powers of manifestation (Shakti).

Having a lifetime's study of profound European thinkers and philosophies behind it, The New Yoga is - in the most literal sense – a European 'reincarnation' of the sublime tradition of tantric teachings known collectively as 'Kashmir Shaivism'. For in the same spirit as its great 10th century adept and teacher – Acharya Abhinavagupta – Acharya Peter Wilberg has again, after a gap of ten centuries, further clarified and refined the principles and practices of this tradition. The New Yoga makes them profoundly relevant to today's world – capable of being applied directly in everyday life and relationships as well as to numerous modern fields of knowledge. That is why, in addition to his many essays and books on The New Yoga, Acharya Peter Wilberg has also contributed several articles to journals of philosophical psychology, written countless essays and published a variety of books on themes ranging from science and religion to medicine and psychiatry, politics and economics, psychoanalysis and psychotherapy.

A COMPARATIVE GLOSSARY OF EXPOSITIONS

This brief glossary relates The Awareness Principle in its new exposition to some of the key Sanskrit terms used in its traditional exposition:

ABHASA – experienced phenomena as 'emanations' or 'manifestations' of awareness

ACHARYA – master and teacher of the precepts of the awareness principle

ADVAITA – 'non-duality' understood as a relation of inseparable distinction

AHAM – the sense of selfhood or 'I'-ness as a primary property of awareness

AHAMKARA - the ego or 'I' that believes that awareness is its private property

AKASHA – 'space' experienced as a spatial field of awareness filled with its 'aether'

AKULA - awareness as transcending the entire group (Kula) of its manifestations

ANANDA – the bliss of identification with the absolute or divine awareness

ANUTTARA – awareness as the 'non-higher', unsurpassable or absolute reality

ATMAN – the self that *is* awareness, the 'experiencing self' or 'awareness self'

BUDDHI – 'mind', 'consciousness'

CHAKRA – centers or 'loci' of awareness

CHITTI – 'contents of consciousness'

CHIT – 'pure awareness' or 'awareness' as such

JIVA – the experienced self in contrast to the experiencing self or awareness self

KARIKAS – collections of or commentaries on basic metaphysical propositions

KARMA – identification with the ego or experienced self, leading to rebirth

KHE/KHA – root of the terms KHAOS or CHAOS (Greek) and KHECHARI (Sanskrit)

KHECHARI – 'moving in the void of space' or 'she who moves in the void' (KHE)

KHECHARI MUDRA – the practice of identification with space

MUDRA – any bodily gesture or comportment that seals a meditative state

NIRVIKALPA – thought-free awareness

PRAKASHA – the light of awareness in which alone all things become manifest

PRANA – the vital 'breath' of awareness (as in 'psyche'/'pneuma'/'anima')

PRATYABHIJNA – recognition of the awareness principle and awareness self

SHAKTI – the feminine aspect of divinity as power of action

SHIVA – the deity personifying absolute subjectivity and the divine awareness

SHIVA-SHAKTI – the relation of awareness (Shiva) to its power of action (Shakti)

SUTRAS – 'threads' in the form of scriptural aphorisms or metaphysical precepts

SVANTANTRYA – the innate freedom belonging to and released by awareness

TANTRA – guarding ('tra') the spreading or expansion ('tan') of awareness

TANTRAS – metaphysical treatises on awareness

TATTVAS – basic qualities of awareness that manifest as experienced phenomena

VIJNANADEHA – the awareness body or body of awareness

VIMARSHA – the mirroring or reflection of the light of awareness the experienced world and in thought or intellectual 'reflection'

YOGA – 'the practice of awareness' aimed at union with the divine awareness through the awareness self (Atman)

Bibliography

Avery, Samuel *The Dimensional Structure of Consciousness* Compari 1995

Dyczkowski, Mark *The Doctrine of Vibration - an Analysis of the Doctrines and Practices of Kashmir Shaivism* State University of New York Press 1987

Feuerstein, Georg *Tantra: The Path of Ecstasy* Shambhala 1998

Feuerstein, Georg *The Yoga Tradition* Hohm Press 2001

Heidegger, Martin *Discourse on Thinking* Harper and Row 1966

Heidegger, Martin *Contributions to Philosophy* Indiana University Press 1999

Husserl, Edmund *The Crisis of the European Sciences and Transcendental Philosophy* Northwestern University Press, 1970

Kosok, Michael *The Singularity of Awareness* Author House 2004

Lawrence, David P. *Rediscovering God with Transcendental Argument* SUNY 1999

Massumi, Brian *A User's Guide to Capitalism and Schizophrenia* MIT 1992

Mehta, J.L. *Philosophy and Religion* Indian Council of Philosophical Research 2004

Muller-Ortega, P.E. *The Triadic Heart of Siva* SUNY Press 1989

Roberts, Jane *Seth Speaks – The Eternal Validity of the Soul* Amber-Allen 1994

SenSharma, Deba Brata *The Philosophy of Sadhana* SUNY Press 1990

Silburn, Lilian *Kundalini – Energy of the Depths* SUNY Press 1988

Singh, Jaideva *Abhinavagupta - Paratrisika-Vivarana* Motilal 2002

Singh, Jaideva *Siva Sutras – The Yoga of Supreme Identity* Motilal 2000

Singh, Jaideva *Spanda-Karikas, The Divine Creative Pulsation* Motilal 2001

Singh, Jaideva *Vijnanabhairava or Divine Consciousness* Motilal 2001

Singh, Jaideva *Pratyabehijnanahrdayam, The Secret of Self-Recognition* Motilal 2003

Shankarananda *The Yoga of Kashmir Shaivism* Motilal 2006

Zimmer, Heinrich *Philosophies of India*, ed. by Joseph Campbell Motilal 1990

Other Books by Peter Wilberg:

Heidegger, Phenomenology and Indian Thought
New Gnosis Publications 2008

The Science Delusion – Why God is Real and Science is Religious Myth
New Gnosis Publications 2008

Tantra Reborn – on the Sensuality and Sexuality of the Soul Body
New Yoga Publications, Exposure Publishing 2007

The New Yoga of Awareness – Tantric Wisdom for Today's World
New Yoga Publications, Exposure Publishing 2007

The Therapist as Listener – Heidegger and the Missing Dimension of Counselling and Psychotherapy Training
New Gnosis Publications 2005

The QUALIA Revolution – from Quantum physics to Qualia Science
New Gnosis Publications 2004

Deep Socialism – A New Manifesto of Marxist Ethics and Economics
New Gnosis Publications 2003

From New Age to New Gnosis – Towards a New Gnostic Spirituality
New Gnosis Publications 2003

Head, Heart and Hara – the Soul Centres of West and East
New Gnosis Publications, 2003

Heidegger, Medicine and 'Scientific Method'
New Gnosis Publications, 2003

22 Conc Vs Awareness

Made in the USA
Lexington, KY
12 September 2013